Ana Sampson

SHE IS FIERCE

Brave, bold and beautiful
poems by women

MACMILLAN

First published 2018 by Macmillan Children's Books
an imprint of Pan Macmillan
20 New Wharf Road, London N1 9RR
Associated companies throughout the world
www.panmacmillan.com

ISBN 978-1-5098-9942-5

A CIP catalogue record for this book is available from
the British Library.

Typeset by The Dimpse
Printed and bound by CPI Group (UK) Ltd, Croydon CR0 4YY

For my daughters

Contents

'We've had a whirl and a blast, girl' – Friendship

'My heart has made its mind up' – Love

'Star-high, heart-deep' – Nature

'I'm glad I exist' – Freedom, Mindfulness and Joy

'Phenomenal woman' – Society, Fashion and Body Image

'But still, like air, I rise' – Courage, Protest and Resistance

'Behind Me – dips Eternity' – Endings

Introduction

It's an exciting time for poetry. Slams and performances are attracting huge audiences; book sales are booming; some of today's biggest online superstars are poets. Women are at the forefront of this movement: winning prizes, headlining festivals, topping bestseller lists and connecting with thousands of readers in digital spaces. It has not always been so.

Anthologies have traditionally been dominated by male voices, seasoned with a mere scattering of women – usually, the same few names. And yet women – wondered at and worshipped by male poets – danced through and dominated those pages. It puzzled me, so I started reading.

Women's songs have always formed a part of oral traditions, though these were often not recorded. Female poets were active in the ancient world but, for the most part, their work was not preserved and some – like Sappho's – was edited or suppressed later. Throughout history and into our own times, women have faced educational, religious and social limitations on their freedom both to write and – especially – to publish. During most eras, it was almost exclusively aristocratic women who had the leisure, learning and liberty to become known as poets.

For centuries it was considered shocking for women to lift their eyes from the housework and seek employment outside the home, and especially for them to trespass in the 'male' arena of literature. Women writers were condemned, or mocked. Parents worried in case potential husbands were put off by their bookish daughters. It has been hard for women – especially if they are also mothers – to find time to work, and to get that work taken seriously. We will never know how many women wrote but didn't dare publish, or exactly how many published under pseudonyms (often men's names), as George Eliot and the Brontë sisters felt that they must.

It was often felt that women should stick to certain subjects – family, friendship, dutiful religion and the prettier corners of nature – and they have written beautifully and powerfully about all these. However, in the poems gathered here and elsewhere, female poets consider every possible subject: science and our magnificent universe; politics and protest; bodies and belief; myths and mental health; war and displacement.

I have included brief biographies of the poets – and what women they were, and are! From suffragettes and freed slaves to schoolgirls, I was fascinated to uncover their stories, many of which were new to me and will, I think, be new to you. Some of these women faced poverty, war, physical and mental illness, oppressive societies and cruelty, but they spun from their experiences wonderful poetry that will speak to readers for generations to come.

Poetry is personal, so any anthology must carry a sincere apology for omissions. I have never found the process of whittling down a longlist more agonizing – there were hundreds of poems loved and lost in the process. I hope you will find in this book a diverse but representative choir of voices – many of which have been unheard for too long – and there will be something unfamiliar and intriguing for every reader. I wish you as much joy reading it as I had compiling it.

Ana Sampson

'My roots spread' – Roots and Growing Up

Here are poems about where – and who – we come from. In some of these verses, the poets explore the notion of home, tracing their own deep roots, and the experience of displacement when those roots are torn up. Others conjure up childhood, from the smell of school to the giddiness of garden games.

Here are sisters: a little Katherine Mansfield fluttering fantasy feathers, and George Eliot movingly mourning her brother's affection after twenty sad years of silence between them. Here are mothers: Sylvia Plath pregnant with promises that must now be kept; Hollie McNish spinning stories about her mysterious baby's midnight adventures; Frances Cornford banishing bedtime terrors. We see them bidding that first farewell at the school gate or the others that come later, when their children fly the nest. And here, too, are daughters: unravelling their futures with a flourish, or sifting the treasures handed down to them by the generations of women that came before.

Diaspora

My roots spread tap and spur from Portugal
the slap, of turquoise seas, on distant sands.
Stems of mine came from ice to Africa
later – to boast a son of Abraham.

I am fertile seed, carried from Ireland
emeralds rich with peat and blue mountain mists.
I am black-work under pomegranate suns
the tale, of a princess of Spain, no less.

Red branches – an envelope, from a new
Chinese uncle. I am a paper dragon
dance, animal years that blossom haiku.
Grown from Gaul leaves, Roman petals sprout words,

Pict, Viking, Saxon, Norman, conquered
with prayer or sword. I am Indian spices
a Maharaja wearing a silk peacock
I am chi, pashmina and pyjamas.

I am every woman, man and small child
in every mirror – puzzles of ancestry
we who call ourselves British, yet as I
sometime   migrants   invaders   refugees.

Sue Hardy-Dawson

To Make a Homeland

Can anyone teach me
how to make a homeland?
Heartfelt thanks if you can,
heartiest thanks,
from the house-sparrows,
the apple-trees of Syria,
and yours very sincerely.

Amineh Abou Kerech

Metaphors

I'm a riddle in nine syllables,
An elephant, a ponderous house,
A melon strolling on two tendrils.
O red fruit, ivory, fine timbers!
This loaf's big with its yeasty rising.
Money's new-minted in this fat purse.
I'm a means, a stage, a cow in calf.
I've eaten a bag of green apples,
Boarded the train there's no getting off.

Sylvia Plath

Milk-Jug Jackers

Baby you look tired, where have you been?
My baby girl smiles gummy and looks up at me.
She says, 'Mummy every morning between midnight and three
We go milk-jug-jacking all my babies and me.
We meet in secret on the green just outside the flats
The babies, bunnies, birds and the cats
We sit on bunnies' backs, galloping, and follow the birds
The cats' eyes light the path of the outside world.
To the big park lakes is where we run
Where, waiting by the piers, are our friendly swans.
We jump off bunnies' backs to the white swans' wings
Sit amongst the feathers where we whisper and sing:
"We are the milk-jug jackers and we're coming your way
Ladies better watch out, put your nipples away
We've got our crowbars at the ready to snap off your straps
Happy slapper milk-jug jackers, hope you're ready for that."
With our animal friends and our bunny-rabbit cars
We sit, snapping bras, in our milk-jug bars
Till our potbellies are full of white baby rum
Then the swans fly us home for our feed time with Mum
Sipping on your nipple I giggle in delight
Cos you don't know I've been drinking milk in all the night.
Sipping on your nipple I giggle in delight
Cos you don't know I've been milk-jug-jacking all of the night.'

Hollie McNish

5

A Glasgow Nonsense Rhyme for Molly

Molly Pin Li McLaren,
come home and look
at the pictures in your brand-new book –
a tree, a bird, a fish, a bell,
a bell, a fish, a tree, a bird.
Point, wee Molly, and say the word!

Oh, Molly, I wish
you the moon as white and round as a dish
and a bell, a tree, a bird and a fish.

Touch! Taste! Look! Smell!
(tree, fish, bird, bell)
And listen, wee Molly, listen well
to the wind,
to the wind in the tree go swish
(bird, bell, tree, fish)
to the shrill of the bird and the plop of the fish
and the clang of the bell
and the stories they tell
the stories they tell,
Molly, the tree, the bird, the fish and the bell.

Liz Lochhead

Ode on the Whole Duty of Parents

The spirits of children are remote and wise,
They must go free
Like fishes in the sea
Or starlings in the skies,
Whilst you remain
The shore where casually they come again.
But when there falls the stalking shade of fear,
You must be suddenly near,
You, the unstable, must become a tree
In whose unending heights of flowering green
Hangs every fruit that grows, with silver bells;
Where heart-distracting magic birds are seen
And all the things a fairy-story tells;
Though still you should possess
Roots that go deep in ordinary earth,
And strong consoling bark
To love and to caress.

Last, when at dark
Safe on the pillow lies an up-gazing head
And drinking holy eyes
Are fixed on you,
When, from behind them, questions come to birth
Insistently,
On all the things that you have ever said
Of suns and snakes and parallelograms and flies,
And whether these are true,
Then for a while you'll need to be no more

That sheltering shore
Or legendary tree in safety spread,
No, then you must put on
The robes of Solomon,
Or simply be
Sir Isaac Newton sitting on the bed.

Frances Cornford

When I Was a Bird

I climbed up the karaka tree
Into a nest all made of leaves
But soft as feathers
I made up a song that went on singing all by itself
And hadn't any words but got sad at the end.
There were daisies in the grass under the tree.
I said, just to try them:
'I'll bite off your heads and give them to my little children to eat.'
But they didn't believe I was a bird
They stayed quite open.
The sky was like a blue nest with white feathers
And the sun was the mother bird keeping it warm.
That's what my song said: though it hadn't any words.
Little Brother came up the path, wheeling his barrow
I made my dress into wings and kept very quiet
Then when he was quite near I said: 'sweet – sweet.'
For a moment he looked quite startled –
Then he said: 'Pooh, you're not a bird; I can see your legs.'
But the daisies didn't really matter
And Little Brother didn't really matter –
I felt *just* like a bird.

Katherine Mansfield

School Parted Us
from Brother and Sister, Sonnet XI

School parted us; we never found again
That childish world where our two spirits mingled
Like scents from varying roses that remain
One sweetness, nor can evermore be singled.
Yet the twin habit of that early time
Lingered for long about the heart and tongue:
We had been natives of one happy clime
And its dear accent to our utterance clung.
Till the dire years whose awful name is Change
Had grasped our souls still yearning in divorce,
And pitiless shaped them in two forms that range
Two elements which sever their life's course.
But were another childhood-world my share,
I would be born a little sister there.

George Eliot

Timetable

We all remember school, of course:
the lino warming, shoe bag smell, expanse
of polished floor. It's where we learned
to wait: hot cheeked in class, dreaming,
bored, for cheesy milk, for noisy now.
We learned to count, to rule off days,
and pattern time in coloured squares:
purple English, dark green Maths.

We hear the bells, sometimes,
for years, the squeal and crack
of chalk on black. We walk, don't run,
in awkward pairs, hoping for the open door,
a foreign teacher, fire drill. And love
is long Aertex summers, tennis sweat,
and somewhere, someone singing flat.
The art room, empty, full of light.

Kate Clanchy

A Glass of Tea

(after Rumi)

Last year, I held a glass of tea to the light. This year,
I swirl like a tealeaf in the streets of Oxford.

Last year, I stared into navy blue sky. This year,
I am roaming under colourless clouds.

Last year, I watched the dazzling sun dance gracefully.
   This year,
The faint sun moves futurelessly.

Migration drove me down this bumpy road,
Where I fell and smelt the soil, where I arose and sensed
   the cloud.

Now I am a bird, flying in the breeze,
Lost over the alien earth.

Don't stop and ask me questions.
Look into my eyes and feel my heart.

It is bruised, aching and sore.
My eyes are veiled with onion skin.

I sit helplessly in an injured nest,
Not knowing how to fix it.

And my heart, I'd say
Is displaced

Struggling to find its place.

Shukria Rezaei

How to Cut a Pomegranate

'Never,' said my father,
'Never cut a pomegranate
through the heart. It will weep blood.
Treat it delicately, with respect.

'Just slit the upper skin across four quarters.
This is a magic fruit,
so when you split it open, be prepared
for the jewels of the world to tumble out,
more precious than garnets,
more lustrous than rubies,
lit as if from inside.
Each jewel contains a living seed.
Separate one crystal.
Hold it up to catch the light.
Inside is a whole universe.
No common jewel can give you this.'

Afterwards, I tried to make necklaces
of pomegranate seeds.
The juice spurted out, bright crimson,
and stained my fingers, then my mouth.
I didn't mind. The juice tasted of gardens
I had never seen, voluptuous
with myrtle, lemon, jasmine,
and alive with parrots' wings.

The pomegranate reminded me
that somewhere I had another home.

Imtiaz Dharker

Bridge

Between here and Colombia
is a pontoon
of fishnet tights filled tight
with star fruit and green, salted mango.

From here to Colombia
is a pageant
of carnivals and parties
and 1 a.m. celebrations and girls
in homemade wedding dresses
twirling on their great-great-uncle's toes.

Between here and Colombia
is a green wave
of parrots tumbling in cages no bigger
than their beady, red-glass eyes.

From here to Colombia
is a necklace
of gourds frothing
with brown nameless soups and fried
everything and big bottom ants and
sauces from everywhere and roadkill armadillo.

Between here and Colombia
is a zip line
of stretched elastic marriages
to high school boy friends.

Between here and Colombia
are stepping stones
of thousands of lost relatives weaving
down hot pavements dangerous with carts
ready to pinch your cheeks and say
You are too thin, what have you been doing?

And I will set out to travel
from here to Colombia
I shall step out
onto the stretched-tight washing line
which links our houses
and wobble on to
the telephone wires
which dangle in the mango trees.
I will ignore the calls
from great-aunts and great-grandmas
great-cousins and first cousins,
and hold out the corners of my dancing skirt.
I shall point my jelly sandals
towards the Colombian sun
and dance *cumbia, cumbia* –

until I get there.

Aisha Borja

I Am My Own Parent

I love my red shoes
all of the shoes I have loved,
they are.

I swing my legs against the wall,
scuffing them slightly.
My dad is not here to pick them up

by the scruffs of their dirty necks
and leave them shining in the morning.
And now, the arc of my swing

is not quite so high,
the shoes every day a little duller.
At night I leave them in the hall like hope.

In the morning,
absentmindedly dreaming of old loves
and reading poetry until it hurts.

I spring suddenly out of bed
and decide to roll up my life into a fist,
smelling of patchouli and roses, and then

unroll it. And to my surprise,
it becomes a snail's yellow shell, unravelling,
On and on it goes. It's gorgeous.

I tap tap my red shoes
to find I'm already home.

Deborah Alma

Huge Blue
(For Jack)

You were three when we moved north,
near the sea. That first time
you took one look, twisted off your clothes
till, bare as the day you were born,

you made off: I had to sprint,
scoop you up just as you threw the whole of you
into its huge blue – or you might be swimming still,
half way to Murmansk, that port you always dreamed of
    seeing:

I once flew, about your age:
strong arms held me hard,
hauled me down so my salted eyelashes
stuck together, sucked blue dark:

I didn't know how to remember
until you opened your arms that day,
sure that the world would hold you
and it did: grown now, and half a world away,

I hope your huge blue
is beautiful with stars
as you leap, eyes wide open,
no ghost of me on your back.

Pippa Little

Song

A scholar first my love implored,
And then an empty titled lord;
The pedant talked in lofty strains;
Alas! his lordship wanted brains:
I listened not to one or t' other,
But straight referred them to my mother.

A poet next my love assailed,
A lawyer hoped to have prevailed;
The bard too much approved himself;
The lawyer thirsted after pelf:
I listened not to one or t' other,
But still referred them to my mother.

An officer my heart would storm,
A miser sought me too, in form,
But Mars was over-free and bold;
The miser's heart was in his gold:
I listened not to one or t' other,
Referring still unto my mother.

And after them, some twenty more
Successless were, as those before;
When Damon, lovely Damon came,
Our hearts straight felt a mutual flame:
I vowed I'd have him, and no other,
Without referring to my mother.

Lady Dorothea Du Bois

To My Daughter On Being Separated from Her on Her Marriage

Dear to my heart as life's warm stream
Which animates this mortal clay,
For thee I court the waking dream,
And deck with smiles the future day;
And thus beguile the present pain
With hopes that we shall meet again.

Yet, will it be as when the past
Twined every joy, and care, and thought,
And o'er our minds one mantle cast
Of kind affections finely wrought?
Ah no! the groundless hope were vain,
For so we ne'er can meet again!

May he who claims thy tender heart
Deserve its love, as I have done!
For, kind and gentle as thou art,
If so beloved, thou art fairly won.
Bright may the sacred torch remain,
And cheer thee till we meet again!

Anne Hunter

Flight Radar

From the top of the Shard the view unfolds
down the Thames to the sea, the city laid
by a trick of sight vertically in front of me.
At London Bridge Station, trains slide in

and out in a long slow dance. It is not
by chance that I am here, not looking down
but up to where you are on Flight 199,
coming in to land. I have learned to track you

on my mobile phone. However far you go,
I have the app that uses the radar to trace
your path. There you are now, circling down
around this spire where I stand, my face reflected

over your pulse in the glass. You cannot see.
You have no radar for me, no app to make you
look back or down to where I am lifting my hand.
Darling, I will track your flight till it is a dot

that turns and banks and falls out of sight, looking
into the space where you were. Fingers frozen
on the tiny keys, I will stay where I am
in the dying light, the screen still live in my palm.

Imtiaz Dharker

Heirloom

She gave me childhood's flowers,
Heather and wild thyme,
Eyebright and tormentil,
Lichen's mealy cup,
Dry on wind-scored stone,
The corbies on the rock,
The rowan by the burn.

Sea marcels a child beheld
Out in the fisherman's boat,
Fringed pulsing violet
Medusa, sea-gooseberries,
Starfish on the sea-floor,
Cowries and rainbow-shells
From pools on a rocky shore.

Gave me her memories,
But kept her last treasure:
'When I was a lass', she said,
'Sitting among the heather,
'Suddenly I saw
'That all the moor was alive!
'I have told no one before.'

That was my mother's tale.
Seventy years had gone
Since she saw the living skein
Of which the world is woven,
And having seen, knew all;
Through long indifferent years
Treasuring the priceless pearl.

Kathleen Raine

Mali

Three years ago to the hour, the day she was born,
that unmistakeable brim and tug of the tide
I'd thought was over. I drove
the twenty miles of summer lanes,
my daughter cursing Sunday cars,
and the lazy swish of a daily herd
rocking so slowly home.

Something in the event,
late summer heat overspilling into harvest,
apples reddening on heavy trees,
the lanes sweet with brambles
and our fingers purple,
then the child coming easy,
too soon, in the wrong place,

things seasonal and out of season
towed home a harvest moon.
My daughter's daughter
a day old under an umbrella on the beach,
Latecomer at summer's festival,
and I'm hooked again, life sentenced.
Even the sea could not draw me from her.

This year I bake her a cake like our house,
and old trees blossom
with balloons and streamers.
We celebrate her with a cup
of cold blue ocean,
candles at twilight, and three drops of,
probably, last blood.

Gillian Clarke

The Pale Horse

At twilight she is still sitting with the book in her hand,
staring through the window, looking for snow.

Have you seen my horse? she says, eyes wild
with loss. I smile, brush her hair. She purrs.

She cups my face. *I know you*, she whispers,
have you stolen my horse? I cover her hands with mine

and we stare a while, nose to nose. *I know you.*
Her lips twitch, try to find the forgotten shape

of my name. I tell her, but she shrugs and turns
to the window, expecting snow.

Lesley Ingram

On Forgetting That I Am a Tree

A poem in which I am growing.

A poem in which I am a tree,
And I am both appreciated and undervalued.

A poem in which I fear I did not dig into the past,
Did not think about my roots,
Forgot what it meant to be planted.

A poem in which I realize they may try to cut me down,
That I must change with the seasons,
That I do it so well
It looks like they are changing with me.

A poem in which I remember I have existed for centuries,
That centuries are far too small a unit of measurement,
That time found itself in the forests, woods and jungles.
Remember I have witnessed creation,
That I am key to it.

A poem in which some will carve their names into my skin
In hopes the universe will know them.
Where I am so tall I kiss the sun.
Trees cannot hide,
They belong to the day and to the night,
To the past and the future.

A poem in which I stop looking for it,
Because I am home.
I am habitat.
My branches are host and shelter
I am life-giver and fruit-bearer.
Self-sufficient protection.

A poem in which I remember I am a tree.

Ruth Awolola

'We've had a whirl and a blast, girl' – Friendship

Some alliances, especially when we are young, have a sharp edge of competition, as seen here in Rhian Edwards's 'Polly' or Kate Tempest's 'Thirteen'. Friendship, as Polly Clark finds, is not always as easy as pop culture promises, though its influence on us is often immense. Throughout our lives, the relationships we forge with our friends are some of the most deep, enduring and important: 'For this,' writes Elizabeth Jennings, 'all Nature slows and sings.'

Here are poems that express the unbeatable feeling of escaping with a partner in crime, from Helen Burke's playtime gallops to Jean Tepperman's yell of girl-gang exhilaration:

'We are screaming,
we are flying,
laughing, and won't stop.'

Here are hymns to long lifetimes of friendship from Jackie Kay and Catherine Maria Fanshawe. Hannah More immortalizes the Bluestockings, gathering in a serene tea-fuelled rebellion to discuss topics considered too challenging for women at the time. Here, too, are poems that remember a glorious shared history, and show long-distance love being sent in letters and even in a fragrant Christmas pudding.

5th Dudley Girl Guides

Your plain faces are lovely as bunting
in the sunlight while you pitch your tents

calling each other to pull guy-ropes taut
crawling easy as lads   lifting

the silver pole inside the green canvas.
I would like to be you again, just for a moment,

catching another wench's smile like a frisbee
raising your flag in the expectant air.

Liz Berry

Thirteen

The boys have football and skate ramps.
They can ride BMX
and play basketball in the courts by the flats until midnight.
The girls have shame.

One day,
when we are grown and we have minds of our own,
we will be kind women, with nice smiles and families and jobs.
And we will sit,
with the weight of our lives and our pain
pushing our bodies down into the bus seats,
and we will see thirteen-year-old girls for what will seem
    like the first time since we've been them,
and they will be sitting in front of us, laughing
into their hands at our shoes or our jackets,
    and rolling their eyes at each other.

While out of the window, in the sunshine,
the boys will be cheering each other on,
and daring each other to jump higher and higher.

Kate Tempest

Lacing Boots

They were narrow, beautiful.
We laced them with finesse.
At lunch hours, pretended we were skaters.
Foreign – mystical enchantresses.

We ran them through the long garden,
down the cinder track, then, through
the wildest stretch, to the tennis courts
and back again.

Folding them, the soft skin doubled over.
Back into our secret locker. In bold
brown brogues we re-appeared
at Latin, double French and Scripture – just as we were
to all around, our feet and hair, neat,
fastened firmly down.
Only ourselves aware that outside two gazelles
were running still,
through the long grass towards
the tennis courts – and on.

Helen Burke

Witch

They told me
I smile prettier with my mouth closed.
They said –
better cut your hair –
long, it's all frizzy,
looks Jewish.
They hushed me in restaurants
looking around them
while the mirrors above the table
jeered infinite reflections
of a raw, square face.
They questioned me
when I sang in the street.
They stood taller at tea
smoothly explaining
my eyes on the saucers,
trying to hide the hand grenade
in my pants pocket,
or crouched behind the piano.
They mocked me with magazines
full of breasts and lace,
published in their triumph
when the doctor's oldest son
married a nice sweet girl.
They told me tweed-suit stories
of various careers of ladies.
I woke up at night

afraid of dying.
They built screens and room dividers
to hide unsightly desire
sixteen years old
raw and hopeless
they buttoned me into dresses
covered with pink flowers.
They waited for me to finish
then continued the conversation.
I have been invisible,
weird and supernatural.
I want my black dress.
I want my hair
curling wild around me.
I want my broomstick
from the closet where I hid it.
Tonight I meet my sisters
in the graveyard.
Around midnight
if you stop at a red light
in the wet city traffic,
watch for us against the moon.
We are screaming,
we are flying,
laughing, and won't stop.

Jean Tepperman

Polly

The gap between your teeth became my ambition,
as did your bias for fountain pens,
rubbing your nose with the ball
of your hand. That succession of clicks
where the bone seemingly turned.
I always wondered at the violence
you gave your cropped hair, yanking a fistful
of it down to your shoulder, a modest trick,
the pretence of decrying yourself
while delivering a lavish answer.

I secretly warred with you in French
and English though never destined
to beat you. Still, we were able to share
the teacher we loved and code-named
Cornelius, as we watched him on Fridays,
buy flowers at the bus station.
We both lived for the pauses
where we composed ghost stories
for each other, promenading the playground,
our arms linked and unbreakable.

How I admired the mess you made,
your massacre of books, the pencilled
note at your bedside, toasting you
for completing *War and Peace*
by the age of eleven. What I wouldn't
have given for your attic scatter,
the names of your sisters,
your fountain pen handwriting, the turgid
lettering I mimicked in secret
and now pass off as my own.

Rhian Edwards

To D.R.

Beyond the bars I see her move,
A mystery of blue and green,
As though across the prison yard
The spirit of the spring had been.
And as she lifts her hands to press
The happy sunshine of her hair,
From the grey ground the pigeons rise,
And rustle upwards in the air,
As though her two hands held a key
To set the imprisoned spirits free.

Laura Grey

To Mrs K., On Her Sending Me an English Christmas Plum-Cake at Paris

What crowding thoughts around me wake,
What marvels in a Christmas-cake!
Ah say, what strange enchantment dwells
Enclosed within its odorous cells?
Is there no small magician bound
Encrusted in its snowy round?
For magic surely lurks in this,
A cake that tells of vanished bliss;
A cake that conjures up to view
The early scenes, when life was new;
When memory knew no sorrows past,
And hope believed in joys that last! –
Mysterious cake, whose folds contain
Life's calendar of bliss and pain;
That speaks of friends for ever fled,
And wakes the tears I love to shed.
Oft shall I breathe her cherished name
From whose fair hand the offering came:
For she recalls the artless smile
Of nymphs that deck my native isle;
Of beauty that we love to trace,
Allied with tender, modest grace;

Of those who, while abroad they roam,
Retain each charm that gladdens home,
And whose dear friendships can impart
A Christmas banquet for the heart!

Helen Maria Williams

Friendship

Such love I cannot analyse;
It does not rest in lips or eyes,
Neither in kisses nor caress.
Partly, I know, it's gentleness

And understanding in one word
Or in brief letters. It's preserved
By trust and by respect and awe.
These are the words I'm feeling for.

Two people, yes, two lasting friends.
The giving comes, the taking ends
There is no measure for such things.
For this all Nature slows and sings.

Elizabeth Jennings

from Essay on Friendship

To Artemisia. – 'Tis to her we sing,
For her once more we touch the founding string.
'Tis not to Cythera's reign nor Cupid's fires,
But sacred Friendship that our muse inspires.
A theme that suits Aemilia's pleasing tongue:
So to the fair ones I devote my song.

The wise will seldom credit all they hear,
Though saucy wits should tell thee with a sneer,
That women's friendships, like a certain fly,
Are hatched i'the morning and at ev'ning die.
'Tis true, our sex has been from early time
A constant topic for satiric rhyme:
Nor without reason – since we're often found
Or lost in passion, or in pleasures drowned:
And the fierce winds that bid the ocean roll
Are less inconstant than a woman's soul:
Yet some there are that keep the mod'rate way,
Can think an hour, and be calm a day:
Who ne'er were known to start into a flame,
Turn pale or tremble at a losing game,
Run Chloe's shape or Delia's features down,
Or change complexion at Celinda's gown:
But still serene, compassionate and kind,
Walk through life's circuit with an equal mind.

Of all companions I would choose to shun
Such, whose blunt truths are like a bursting gun,
Who in a breath count all your follies o'er,
And close their lectures with a mirthful roar:
But reason here will prove the safest guide,
Extremes are dang'rous placed on either side.
A friend too soft will hardly prove sincere;
The wit's inconstant, and the learn'd severe.
Good breeding, wit, and learning, all conspire
To charm mankind and make the world admire,
Yet in a friend but serve an under part:
The main ingredient is an honest heart.

Mary Leapor

Friends

It showed how friendship
doesn't end (like when
Emma and I watched

eight episodes in one go)
though outside my window
the climate was changing

and in my experience
people found each other
quite easy to take or leave.

The day after the last episode
they ran them all again,
protecting me, it seems.

I keep just one from
two-hundred-and-thirty-six.
It's the one where Ross says,

but this can't be it,
and Rachel says,
then how come it is?

and he sinks to his knees with his arms
around her legs and the camera
moves slowly back

and they hold the shot
for a long time
before the theme tune begins.

Polly Clark

from The Bas Bleu

Hail, Conversation, soothing power,
Sweet goddess of the social hour!
O may thy worship long prevail,
And thy true votaries never fail!
Long may thy polished altars blaze
With wax-lights' undiminished rays!
Still be thy nightly offerings paid,
Libations large of lemonade!
In silver vases, loaded, rise
The biscuits' ample sacrifice!
Nor be the milk-white streams forgot
Of thirst-assuaging, cool orgeat;
Rise, incense pure from fragrant tea,
Delicious incense, worthy thee!

Hannah More

Introductions

Some of what we love
we stumble upon –
a purse of gold thrown on the road,
a poem, a friend, a great song.

And more
discloses itself to us –
a well among green hazels,
a nut thicket –
when we are worn out searching
for something quite different.

And more
comes to us, carried
as carefully
as a bright cup of water,
as new bread.

Moya Cannon

When Last We Parted

When last we parted, thou wert young and fair,
How beautiful let fond remembrance say!
Alas! since then old time has stolen away
Full thirty years, leaving my temples bare. –
So has it perished like a thing of air,
The dream of love and youth! – now both are grey
Yet still remembering that delightful day,
Though time with his cold touch has blanched my hair,
Though I have suffered many years of pain
Since then, though I did never think to live
To hear that voice or see those eyes again,
I can a sad but cordial greeting give,
And for thy welfare breathe as warm a prayer –
As when I loved thee young and fair.

Catherine Maria Fanshawe

Long Departure

Then I said to the elegant ladies:
'How you will remember when you are old
the glorious things we did in our youth!

We did many pure and beautiful things.
Now that you are leaving the city,
love's sharp pain encircles my heart.'

Sappho

Fiere

If ye went tae the tapmost hill, Fiere
Whaur we used tae clamb as girls,
Ye'd see the snow the day, Fiere,
Settling on the hills.
You'd mind o' anither day, mibbe,
We ran doon the hill in the snow,
Sliding and singing oor way tae the foot,
Lassies laughing thegither – how braw.
The years slipping awa; oot in the weather.

And noo we're suddenly auld, Fiere,
Oor friendship's ne'er been weary.
We've aye seen the wurld differently.
Whaur would I hae been weyoot my jo,
My fiere, my fiercy, my dearie O?
Oor hair micht be silver noo,
Oor walk a wee bit doddery,
But we've had a whirl and a blast, girl,
Thru' the cauld blast winter, thru spring, summer.

O'er a lifetime, my fiere, my bonnie lassie,
I'd defend you – you, me; blithe and blatter,
Here we gang doon the hill, nae matter,
Past the bracken, bothy, bonny braes, barley.
Oot by the roaring Sea, still havin a blether.
We who loved sincerely; we who loved sae fiercely.
The snow ne'er looked sae barrie,
Nor the winter trees sae pretty.
C'mon, c'mon my dearie – tak my hand, my fiere!

Jackie Kay

'My heart has made its mind up' – Love

Love has always preoccupied poets. Most anthologies are stuffed with goddesses. Glimpsed but not grasped, they are the idealized objects of breathless infatuation immortalized by, usually, male writers. Christina Rossetti and Elizabeth Siddal answer that stereotype sharply here. The artist – in this case, Dante Gabriel Rossetti, brother to one and husband to the other – feeds on his misunderstood muse, worshipping her face while ignoring her feelings.

These verses – addressed to both men and women – speak of heart-stopping moments when eyes meet, fencing foils clash and smartphones glow. The extravagant thrill of new love floods poems by Jenny Joseph, Astrid Hjertenaes Andersen and – in one of the best-loved and most famous poems ever written – Elizabeth Barrett Browning. Women have written especially beautifully about what can rise from the embers of passion: long-lasting love, tender and content, and there are fine examples here from Amy Lowell and Louise Bogan. But there are also poems here about love's difficulties – the need for reconciliation and forgiveness, the frustration of familiarity and the sting of betrayal – as well as words that will comfort anyone who has loved and lost.

Phosphorescence

Record this you say and I'm left
in the shallows, holding your phone.

And I capture it all – the moon
low and lush as a forbidden fruit,

you, striking light after light
as you cross the bay, the way

your face, as you turn to wave,
is star-varnished like that of a god.

Before you upload, before the flurry
of *likes* for this phenomenon,

there's a moment when your world
is gleaming in my hands. Tonight

I would gulp down this blooming ocean
for a taste of your skin.

Victoria Gatehouse

Practice

As a teenager, fencing was the closest thing
I knew to desire, all the girls swapping one

> uniform for another before practice, their white
> dresses replaced by breeches. I thought we were

princes in a fairy tale with a twist, since
there were no princesses to be taken, wed.

> As knights, we were told to aim for an imaginary
> spot just above our opponent's left breast. Often,

I left a bruise: the blade's tip ricocheting off chest-
guards on to flesh. Just as often, I would feel yellow

> blooms of ache where the girl I thought was beautiful
> had pierced my heart. Hours later, I would transform.

I would head back home with a deepening
sense of dread, my bruises fading to quiet.

Mary Jean Chan

A Pride of Ladies

They wore light dresses and their arms were bare,
paddling backwater seasons, moonstruck, coy,
who cooled their necks with pale green spicy scents
and spread skirts stiff in petals as they sat
dazzled, waiting becalmed; and one might lift
hair bright as buglings on the wind.
All princesses.

And someone came, or would come soon enough
whose common words were stranger than the spell;
whose quick and faintly furry hand might not
fit those curved palms; would have been glad to stay
stretched flat, count polished pebbles, wait, and sun
a young brown back, pretending to be earth.

And not a prince. His breath was dark and sour.
He was not tall. But he was chosen. Chose,
and so must come, perhaps in the new moon.
Awkward himself, and shy, would learn to be
Mariner, Swineherd, King,
and set one free.

Anne Halley

Siren Song

This is the one song everyone
would like to learn: the song
that is irresistible:

the song that forces men
to leap overboard in squadrons
even though they see the beached skulls

the song nobody knows
because anyone who has heard it
is dead, and the others can't remember.

Shall I tell you the secret
and if I do, will you get me
out of this bird suit?

I don't enjoy it here
squatting on this island
looking picturesque and mythical

with these two feathery maniacs,
I don't enjoy singing
this trio, fatal and valuable.

I will tell the secret to you,
to you, only to you.
Come closer. This song

is a cry for help: Help me!
Only you, only you can,
you are unique

at last. Alas
it is a boring song
but it works every time.

Margaret Atwood

Valentine

Not a red rose or a satin heart.

I give you an onion.
It is a moon wrapped in brown paper.
It promises light
like the careful undressing of love.

Here.
It will blind you with tears
like a lover.
It will make your reflection
a wobbling photo of grief.

I am trying to be truthful.

Not a cute card or a kissogram.

I give you an onion.
Its fierce kiss will stay on your lips,
possessive and faithful
as we are,
for as long as we are.

Take it.
Its platinum loops shrink to a wedding ring,
if you like.
Lethal.
Its scent will cling to your fingers,
cling to your knife.

Carol Ann Duffy

A Moment

The clouds had made a crimson crown
  Above the mountains high.
The stormy sun was going down
  In a stormy sky.

Why did you let your eyes so rest on me,
  And hold your breath between?
In all the ages this can never be
  As if it had not been.

Mary Elizabeth Coleridge

In an Artist's Studio

One face looks out from all his canvases,
   One selfsame figure sits or walks or leans:
   We found her hidden just behind those screens,
That mirror gave back all her loveliness.
A queen in opal or in ruby dress,
   A nameless girl in freshest summer-greens,
   A saint, an angel — every canvas means
The same one meaning, neither more nor less.
He feeds upon her face by day and night,
   And she with true kind eyes looks back on him,
Fair as the moon and joyful as the light:
   Not wan with waiting, not with sorrow dim;
Not as she is, but was when hope shone bright;
   Not as she is, but as she fills his dream.

Christina Rossetti

The Lust of the Eyes

I care not for my Lady's soul,
    Though I worship before her smile:
I care not where be my Lady's goal
    When her beauty shall lose its wile.

Low sit I down at my Lady's feet,
    Gazing through her wild eyes,
Smiling to think how my love will fleet
    When their starlike beauty dies.

I care not if my Lady pray
    To our Father which is in Heaven;
But for joy my heart's quick pulses play,
    For to me her love is given.

Then who shall close my Lady's eyes,
    And who shall fold her hands?
Will any hearken if she cries
    Up to the unknown lands?

Elizabeth Siddal

The Guitarist Tunes Up

With what attentive courtesy he bent

Over his instrument;
Not as a lordly conqueror who could

Command both wire and wood,
But as a man with a loved woman might,

Inquiring with delight
What slight essential things she had to say
Before they started, he and she, to play.

Frances Cornford

Before the sun goes down

Before the sun goes down

I'll lay my wildflower hand
in your hand's white wicker basket

and bold – tender – shy I'll encircle you
as day and night would encircle
the trees of the day and night

and my kisses will live like birds on your shoulder

Astrid Hjertenaes Andersen

Translated by Nadia Christensen

Sonnet 43

How do I love thee? Let me count the ways.
I love thee to the depth and breadth and height
My soul can reach, when feeling out of sight
For the ends of Being and ideal Grace.
I love thee to the level of everyday's
Most quiet need, by sun and candle-light.
I love thee freely, as men strive for Right;
I love thee purely, as they turn from Praise.
I love thee with the passion put to use
In my old griefs, and with my childhood's faith.
I love thee with a love I seemed to lose
With my lost saints – I love thee with the breath,
Smiles, tears, of all my life! – and, if God choose,
I shall but love thee better after death.

Elizabeth Barrett Browning

A Birthday

My heart is like a singing bird
   Whose nest is in a watered shoot;
My heart is like an apple-tree
   Whose boughs are bent with thickest fruit;
My heart is like a rainbow shell
   That paddles in a halcyon sea;
My heart is gladder than all these
   Because my love is come to me.

Raise me a dais of silk and down;
   Hang it with vair and purple dyes;
Carve it in doves, and pomegranates,
   And peacocks with a hundred eyes;
Work it in gold and silver grapes,
   In leaves, and silver fleurs-de-lys;
Because the birthday of my life
   Is come, my love is come to me.

Christina Rossetti

The Sun Has Burst the Sky

The sun has burst the sky
Because I love you
And the river its banks.

The sea laps the great rocks
Because I love you
And takes no heed of the moon dragging it away
And saying coldly 'Constancy is not for you'.
The blackbird fills the air
Because I love you
With spring and lawns and shadows falling on lawns.

The people walk in the street and laugh
I love you
And far down the river ships sound their hooters
Crazy with joy because I love you.

Jenny Joseph

The house was just twinkling in the moon light

The house was just twinkling in the moon light,
And inside it twinkling with delight,
Is my baby bright.
Twinkling with delight in the house twinkling
with the moonlight,
Bless my baby bless my baby bright,
Bless my baby twinkling with delight,
In the house twinkling in the moon light,
Her hubby dear loves to cheer when he thinks
and he always thinks when he knows and he always
knows that his blessed baby wifey is all here and he
is all hers, and sticks to her like burrs, blessed baby

Gertrude Stein

Reconciliation

Into my lap, a great star will fall . . .
we would keep watch at night,

praying in languages
carved like harps,

We would make our peace with the night –
so much of God flows through it.

Our hearts are like children,
wanting sleepsweet rest.

And our lips want to kiss,
so what makes you hold back?

Does my heart not border on yours,
your blood not redden my cheek?

We would make our peace with the night,
and if we embrace, we will not die.

Into my lap, a great star will fall.

Else Lasker-Schüler

Translated by James Sheard

Camomile Tea

Outside the sky is light with stars;
There's a hollow roaring from the sea.
And, alas! for the little almond flowers,
The wind is shaking the almond tree.

How little I thought, a year ago,
In the horrible cottage upon the Lee,
That he and I should be sitting so
And sipping a cup of camomile tea.

Light as feathers the witches fly,
The horn of the moon is plain to see;
By a firefly under a jonquil flower
A goblin toasts a bumble-bee.

We might be fifty, we might be five,
So snug, so compact, so wise are we!
Under the kitchen-table leg
My knee is pressing against his knee.

Katherine Mansfield

To my Dear and Loving Husband

If ever two were one, then surely we.
If ever man were loved by wife, then thee;
If ever wife was happy in a man,
Compare with me ye women if you can.
I prize thy love more than whole mines of gold,
Or all the riches that the East doth hold.
My love is such that rivers cannot quench,
Nor ought but love from thee give recompense.
Thy love is such I can no way repay;
The heavens reward thee manifold, I pray.
Then while we live, in love let's so persever,
That when we live no more we may live ever.

Anne Bradstreet

A Decade

When you came, you were like red wine and honey,
And the taste of you burnt my mouth with its sweetness.
Now you are like morning bread,
Smooth and pleasant.
I hardly taste you at all for I know your savour,
But I am completely nourished.

Amy Lowell

Wedding

From time to time our love is like a sail
and when the sail begins to alternate
from tack to tack, it's like a swallowtail
and when the swallow flies it's like a coat;
and if the coat is yours, it has a tear
like a wide mouth and when the mouth begins
to draw the wind, it's like a trumpeter
and when the trumpet blows, it blows like millions . . .
and this, my love, when millions come and go
beyond the need of us, is like a trick;
and when the trick begins, it's like a toe
tiptoeing on a rope, which is like luck;
and when the luck begins, it's like a wedding,
which is like love, which is like everything.

Alice Oswald

Anniversary

Suppose I took out a slender ketch from
under the spokes of Palace pier tonight to
catch a sea going fish for you

or dressed in antique goggles and wings and
flew down through sycamore leaves into the park

or luminescent through some planetary strike
put one delicate flamingo leg over the sill of your lab

Could I surprise you?   or would you insist on
keeping a pattern to link every transfiguration?

Listen, I shall have to whisper it
into your heart directly: we are all
supernatural / every day
we rise new creatures / cannot be predicted

Elaine Feinstein

Song for the Last Act

Now that I have your face by heart, I look
Less at its features than its darkening frame
Where quince and melon, yellow as young flame,
Lie with quilled dahlias and the shepherd's crook.
Beyond, a garden. There, in insolent ease
The lead and marble figures watch the show
Of yet another summer loath to go
Although the scythes hang in the apple trees.

Now that I have your face by heart, I look.

Now that I have your voice by heart, I read
In the black chords upon a dulling page
Music that is not meant for music's cage,
Whose emblems mix with words that shake and bleed.
The staves are shuttled over with a stark
Unprinted silence. In a double dream
I must spell out the storm, the running stream.
The beat's too swift. The notes shift in the dark.

Now that I have your voice by heart, I read.

'My heart has made its mind up' – Love

Now that I have your heart by heart, I see
The wharves with their great ships and architraves;
The rigging and the cargo and the slaves
On a strange beach under a broken sky.
O not departure, but a voyage done!
The bales stand on the stone; the anchor weeps
Its red rust downward, and the long vine creeps
Beside the salt herb, in the lengthening sun.

Now that I have your heart by heart, I see.

Louise Bogan

Kissing

The young are walking on the riverbank
arms around each other's waist and shoulders,
pretending to be looking at the waterlilies
and what might be a nest of some kind, over
there, which two who are clamped together
mouth to mouth have forgotten about.
The others, making courteous detours
around them, talk, stop talking, kiss.
They can see no one older than themselves.
It's their river. They've got all day.

Seeing's not everything. At this very
moment the middle-aged are kissing
in the backs of taxis, on the way
to airports and stations. Their mouths and tongues
are soft and powerful and as moist as ever.
Their hands are not inside each other's clothes
(because of the driver) but locked so tightly
together that it hurts: it may leave marks
on their not of course youthful skin, which they won't
notice. They too may have futures.

Fleur Adcock

Renouncement

I must not think of thee; and, tired yet strong,
I shun the thought that lurks in all delight –
The thought of thee – and in the blue heaven's height,
And in the sweetest passage of a song.
O just beyond the fairest thoughts that throng
This breast, the thought of thee waits, hidden yet bright;
But it must never, never come in sight;
I must stop short of thee the whole day long.
But when sleep comes to close each difficult day,
When night gives pause to the long watch I keep,
And all my bonds I needs must loose apart,
And doff my will as raiment laid away, –
With the first dream that comes with the first sleep,
I run, I run, I am gathered to thy heart.

Alice Meynell

Among His Books

A silent room – grey with a dusty blight
    Of loneliness;
A room with not enough of light
    Its form to dress.

Books enough though! The groaning sofa bears
    A goodly store –
Books on the window-seat, and on the chairs,
    And on the floor.

Books of all sorts of soul, all sorts of age,
    All sorts of face –
Black-letter, vellum, and the flimsy page
    Of commonplace.

All bindings, from the cloth whose hue distracts
    One's weary nerves,
To yellow parchment, binding rare old tracts
    It serves – deserves.

Books on the shelves, and in the cupboard books,
    Worthless and rare –
Books on the mantelpiece – wheree'er one looks
    Books everywhere!

Books! books! the only things in life I find
      Not wholly vain.
Books in my hands – books in my heart enshrined –
      Books in my brain.

My friends are they: for children and for wife
      They serve me too;
For these alone, of all dear things in life,
      Have I found true.

They do not flatter, change, deny, deceive –
      Ah no – not they!
The same editions which one night you leave
      You find next day.

You don't find railway novels where you left
      Your Elzevirs!
Your Aldines don't betray you – leave bereft
      Your lonely years!

And yet this common book of Common Prayer
      My heart prefers,
Because the names upon the fly-leaf there
      Are mine and hers.

It's a dead flower that makes it open so –
      Forget-me-not –
The Marriage Service . . . well, my dear, you know
      Who first forgot.

Those were the days when in the choir we two
      Sat – used to sing –
When I believed in God, in love, in you –
      In everything.

Through quiet lanes to church we used to come,
      Happy and good,
Clasp hands through sermon, and go slowly home
      Down through the wood.

Kisses? A certain yellow rose no doubt
      That porch still shows,
Whenever I hear kisses talked about
      I smell that rose!

No – I don't blame you – since you only proved
      My choice unwise,
And taught me books should trusted be and loved.
      Not lips and eyes!

And so I keep your book – your flower – to show
      How much I care
For the dear memory of what, you know,
      You never were.

Edith Nesbit

Why?

Why did you come, with your enkindled eyes
And mountain-look, across my lower way.
And take the vague dishonour from my day
By luring me from paltry things, to rise
And stand beside you, waiting wistfully
The looming of a larger destiny?

Why did you with strong fingers fling aside
The gates of possibility, and say
With vital voice the words I dream to-day?
Before, I was not much unsatisfied:
But since a god has touched me and departed,
I run through every temple, broken-hearted.

Mary Webb

Love Comes Back

Like your father,
twenty years later with the packet of cigarettes he went
  out for
Like Monday but this is the nineteenth century
& you're a monied aristocrat with no conception of the
  working week

Like a haunted board game
pried from the rubble of an archaeological dig site
You roll the dice & bats come flooding out your heart
like molten grappling hooks
your resolve weakening . . .
like the cord of an antique disco ball . . .

Love like the recurring decimal of some huge, indivisible
  number
or a well thrown boomerang
coming to rest in the soft curve of your hand

Love comes back . . .
like a murderer returning to the scene of the crime . . .
or not returning . . .
yet still the crime remains . . .
like love . . .
observed or unobserved . . .
written in blood on the walls of some ancient civilisation
in an idiom so old
we have no contemporary vernacular equivalent

Love like Windows 95
The greatest, most user-friendly Windows of them all
Those four little panes of light
Like the stained glass of an ancient church
vibrating in the sunlit rubble
of the twentieth century

Your face comes floating up in my crystal ball . . .

The lights come on at the bottom of the ocean
& here we are alone again . . .

Late November
we ride the black escalator of the mountain
& emerge into the altitude of our last year
The rabbit in the grass gives us something wild to aim for
It twists into spring like a living bell

I have to be here always telling you that
no matter how far I travel beyond you
love will stay tethered
like an evil kite I want to always reel back in
As if we could just turn and wade back
through the ghost of some ancient season
or wake each morning in the heat of a vanished life

Love comes back
from where it's never gone . . . It was here the whole time
like a genetic anomaly waiting to reveal itself
Like spring at the museum, after centuries of silence
the bronze wings of gladiator helmets trembling in their
   sockets . . .
Grecian urns sprouting new leaves . . .

Love like a hand from the grave
trembling up into the sunlight of the credit sequence
the names of the dead
pouring down the screen
like cool spring rain

Hera Lindsay Bird

heat

I miss you in tiny earthquakes.
In little underground explosions.
My soil is a hot disaster.
Home is burning.
You're a lost thing.

Yrsa Daley-Ward

One Art

The art of losing isn't hard to master;
so many things seem filled with the intent
to be lost that their loss is no disaster.

Lose something every day. Accept the fluster
of lost door keys, the hour badly spent.
The art of losing isn't hard to master.

Then practise losing farther, losing faster:
places, and names, and where it was you meant
to travel. None of these will bring disaster.

I lost my mother's watch. And look! my last, or
next-to-last, of three loved houses went.
The art of losing isn't hard to master.

I lost two cities, lovely ones. And, vaster,
some realms I owned, two rivers, a continent.
I miss them, but it wasn't a disaster.

— Even losing you (the joking voice, a gesture
I love) I shan't have lied. It's evident
the art of losing's not too hard to master
though it may look like (*Write* it!) like disaster.

Elizabeth Bishop

Dead Love

Oh never weep for love that's dead,
    Since love is seldom true,
But changes his fashion from blue to red,
    From brightest red to blue,
And love was born to an early death
    And is so seldom true.

Then harbour no smile on your loving face
    To win the deepest sigh;
The fairest words on truest lips
    Pass off and surely die;
And you will stand alone, my dear,
    When wintry winds draw nigh.

Sweet, never weep for what cannot be,
    For this God has not given:
If the merest dream of love were true,
    Then, sweet, we should be in heaven;
And this is only earth, my dear,
    Where true love is not given.

Elizabeth Siddal

Let It Be Forgotten

Let it be forgotten, as a flower is forgotten,
Forgotten as a fire that once was singing gold,
Let it be forgotten for ever and ever,
Time is a kind friend, he will make us old.

If anyone asks, say it was forgotten
Long and long ago
As a flower, as a fire, as a hushed footfall
In a long forgotten snow.

Sara Teasdale

'Star-high, heart-deep' – Nature

Women have written many wonderful poems about the natural world but I discovered fewer than I had expected, especially from earlier times. There have certainly been periods in history when it must have been difficult and unusual for women to tramp around the countryside as men have always done: alone, wearing sensible shoes and seeking inspiration in wild and free places. I also had to wonder whether the many gorgeous moonlit poems I discovered existed because those were the only moments the poet could snatch for herself, as the family lay sleeping.

This is a joyful collection of poems about shell-studded coastlines, deep green woods and – of course – the Brontës' beloved Yorkshire moors. From the rolling hills of England, to the tiger-haunted Bangladeshi forest and starry New Zealand skies, these verses have the power to transport and delight. Here, too, are beasts brought to vivid life: a wild hare, a shorn sheep and even Thibault the lobster, pet of the poet Gérard de Nerval, who was looped with a blue ribbon and taken for walks through nineteenth-century Paris.

The Awakening River

The gulls are mad-in-love with the river
And the river unveils her face and smiles.
In her sleep-brooding eyes they mirror their shining wings.
She lies on silver pillows: the sun leans over her.
He warms and warms her, he kisses and kisses her.
There are sparks in her hair and she stirs in laughter.
Be careful, my beautiful waking one! you will catch on fire.
Wheeling and flying with the foam of the sea on their breasts
The ineffable mists of the sea clinging to their wild wings
Crying the rapture of the boundless ocean.
The gulls are mad-in-love with the river.
Wake! we are the dream thoughts flying from your heart.
Wake! we are the songs of desire flowing from your bosom.
O, I think the sun will lend her his great wings
And the river will fly away to the sea with the mad-in-love birds.

Katherine Mansfield

High Waving Heather

High waving heather, 'neath stormy blasts bending,
Midnight and moonlight and bright shining stars;
Darkness and glory rejoicingly blending,
Earth rising to heaven and heaven descending,
Man's spirit away from its drear dongeon sending,
Bursting the fetters and breaking the bars.

All down the mountain sides, wild forest lending
One mighty voice to the life-giving wind;
Rivers their banks in the jubilee rending,
Fast through the valleys a reckless course wending,
Wider and deeper their waters extending,
Leaving a desolate desert behind.

Shining and lowering and swelling and dying,
Changing for ever from midnight to noon;
Roaring like thunder, like soft music sighing,
Shadows on shadows advancing and flying,
Lightning-bright flashes the deep gloom defying,
Coming as swiftly and fading as soon.

Emily Brontë

Address to a Child During a Boisterous Winter Evening

What way does the wind come? What way does he go?
He rides over the water, and over the snow,
Through wood, and through vale; and o'er rocky height,
Which the goat cannot climb, takes his sounding flight;
He tosses about in every bare tree,
As, if you look up, you plainly may see;
But how he will come, and whither he goes,
There's never a scholar in England knows.

He will suddenly stop in a cunning nook,
And ring a sharp 'larum; but, if you should look,
There's nothing to see but a cushion of snow,
Round as a pillow, and whiter than milk,
And softer than if it were covered with silk.
Sometimes he'll hide in the cave of a rock,
Then whistle as shrill as the buzzard cock;
– Yet seek him, and what shall you find in the place?
Nothing but silence and empty space;
Save, in a corner, a heap of dry leaves,
That he's left, for a bed, to beggars or thieves!

As soon as 'tis daylight tomorrow, with me
You shall go to the orchard, and then you will see
That he has been there, and made a great rout,
And cracked the branches, and strewn them about;
Heaven grant that he spare but that one upright twig

That looked up at the sky so proud and big
All last summer, as well you know,
Studded with apples, a beautiful show!

Hark! over the roof he makes a pause,
And growls as if he would fix his claws
Right in the slates, and with a huge rattle
Drive them down, like men in a battle:
– But let him range round; he does us no harm,
We build up the fire, we're snug and warm;
Untouched by his breath see the candle shines bright,
And burns with a clear and steady light.

Books have we to read, but that half-stifled knell,
Alas! 'tis the sound of the eight o'clock bell.
– Come, now we'll to bed! and when we are there
He may work his own will, and what shall we care?
He may knock at the door – we'll not let him in;
May drive at the windows – we'll laugh at his din;
Let him seek his own home wherever it be;
Here's a *cozie* warm house for Edward and me.

Dorothy Wordsworth

Lines Composed in a Wood on a Windy Day

My soul is awakened, my spirit is soaring
   And carried aloft on the wings of the breeze;
For above and around me the wild wind is roaring,
   Arousing to rapture the earth and the seas.

The long withered grass in the sunshine is glancing,
   The bare trees are tossing their branches on high;
The dead leaves beneath them are merrily dancing,
   The white clouds are scudding across the blue sky.

I wish I could see how the ocean is lashing
   The foam of its billows to whirlwinds of spray;
I wish I could see how its proud waves are dashing,
   And hear the wild roar of their thunder to-day!

Anne Brontë

Breakage

I go down to the edge of the sea.
How everything shines in the morning light!
The cusp of the whelk,
the broken cupboard of the clam,
the opened, blue mussels,
moon snails, pale pink and barnacle scarred—
and nothing at all whole or shut, but tattered, split,
dropped by the gulls onto the gray rocks and all the
   moisture gone.
It's like a schoolhouse
of little words,
thousands of words.
First you figure out what each one means by itself,
the jingle, the periwinkle, the scallop
   full of moonlight.

Then you begin, slowly, to read the whole story.

Mary Oliver

The Trees' Counselling

I was strolling sorrowfully
  Thro' the corn fields and the meadows;
The stream sounded melancholy,
  And I walked among the shadows;
While the ancient forest trees
Talked together in the breeze;
In the breeze that waved and blew them,
With a strange weird rustle thro' them.

Said the oak unto the others
  In a leafy voice and pleasant:
'Here we all are equal brothers,
  'Here we have nor lord nor peasant
'Summer, Autumn, Winter, Spring,
'Pass in happy following.
'Little winds may whistle by us,
'Little birds may overfly us;

'But the sun still waits in heaven
  'To look down on us in splendour;
'When he goes the moon is given,
  'Full of rays that he doth lend her:
'And tho' sometimes in the night
'Mists may hide her from our sight,
'She comes out in the calm weather,
'With the glorious stars together.'

From the fruitage, from the blossom,
    From the trees came no denying;
Then my heart said in my bosom:
    'Wherefore art thou sad and sighing?
'Learn contentment from this wood
'That proclaimeth all states good;
'Go not from it as it found thee;
'Turn thyself and gaze around thee.'

And I turned: behold the shading
    But showed forth the light more clearly;
The wild bees were honey-lading;
    The stream sounded hushing merely,
And the wind not murmuring
Seemed, but gently whispering:
'Get thee patience; and thy spirit
'Shall discern in all things merit.'

Christina Rossetti

The Unseen Life of Trees
(For Esther and Jess)

When the fraying skeins of silver birch
sway in the wind they think of
lulling water in the floating harbour,

the dried out plants on a deck,
the bespoke barge door cut to close
on a trapezium.

A sparse beech globe of yellow
holds an afternoon with two young friends,
who will walk through their vivid lives

beyond the end of mine.
A ball of mistletoe hangs
way up in spindle branches balancing

a trowel, a ginger cake,
and a framed copy of Jessop's 1802
'Design for Improving the Harbour of Bristol'.

Umber banks of oak climb the hillside
dragging children by the hand.
'There will be time,' they whisper,

canopy to canopy.
'There will be time, before
all our leaves stretch out across the frosted ground.'

Chrissie Gittins

Green Rain

Into the scented woods we'll go,
And see the blackthorn swim in snow.
High above, in the budding leaves,
A brooding dove awakes and grieves;
The glades with mingled music stir,
And wildly laughs the woodpecker.
When blackthorn petals pearl the breeze,
There are the twisted hawthorn trees
Thick-set with buds, as clear and pale
As golden water or green hail –
As if a storm of rain had stood
Enchanted in the thorny wood,
And, hearing fairy voices call,
Hung poised, forgetting how to fall.

Mary Webb

from Aurora Leigh

But then the thrushes sang,
And shook my pulses and the elms' new leaves . . .
I flattered all the beauteous country round,
As poets use; the skies, the clouds, the fields,
The happy violets hiding from the roads
The primroses run down to, carrying gold, –
The tangled hedgerows, where the cows push out
Impatient horns and tolerant churning mouths
'Twixt dripping ash-boughs, – hedgerows all alive
With birds and gnats and large white butterflies
Which look as if the May-flower had caught life
And palpitated forth upon the wind, –
Hills, vales, woods, netted in a silver mist,
Farms, granges, doubled up among the hills,
And cattle grazing in the watered vales,
And cottage-chimneys smoking from the woods,
And cottage-gardens smelling everywhere,
Confused with smell of orchards.

Elizabeth Barrett Browning

For Forest

Forest could keep secrets
Forest could keep secrets

Forest tune in every day
to watersound and birdsound
Forest letting her hair down
to the teeming creeping of her forest-ground

But Forest don't broadcast her business
no Forest cover her business down
from sky and fast-eye sun
and when night come
and darkness wrap her like a gown
Forest is a bad dream woman

Forest dreaming about mountain
and when earth was young
Forest dreaming of the caress of gold
Forest roosting with mysterious eldorado
and when howler monkey
wake her up with howl
Forest just stretch and stir
to a new day of sound

but coming back to secrets
Forest could keep secrets
Forest could keep secrets
And we must keep Forest

Grace Nichols

Sylhet

There,
Sun birds chipper,
Their feathers, light lime,
Seep in the sunshine.

Crisp leaves grow,
Wild and olive,
And the silent streams
Run,

Fresh water,
To guide the Elish,
Silver, simple fish,
Away to the sea.

Mango trees
Summit and soar,
Stalk high above
The forest floor.

Where
A Bengal tiger,
Obsolete
As an emperor

Trembles
As the hushed wind –
Breathes –

Rukiya Khatun

How to knit a sheep

Start with the legs. It helps to
grab a hoof before casting on, or
he might kick you off. Hold the yarn
taut enough to test his strength,
loose enough to feel his flank quiver
as he bunches shanks to stretch the
ply, hoping it will fray. Loop and dip,
add sufficient stitches to keep his
interest, praise his beauty while
you unravel him, tug gently or he'll
slip your noose. Twist and roll, turn
and back again, keep your palm
against his side as you slide the pins
around about, each click a kiss,
each gartered purl a sweet low
riff to make him give it all, slough
that fleece in one soft piece
to flow from fingertips to floor.
Scoop it up and sniff warm oil
rising through his staple, the crop
he gives up now with grace. Keep
your face pressed to his curls,
breathe the heat and wax of him
behind his ears as hands move
faster as you near the end, his chest

bare and cold, your feet hot under
so much weight. Tie the ends off tight
before you let him go, your nose to his
in thanks only eskimos understand.

Di Slaney

Nerval and the Lobster

His beautiful clatter turns heads.
I explain: he does not bark.
He knows the secrets of the sea.

He is docile at my heel
and slender as a mayfly.
He moves like a long blue bone.

I ask: what are you thinking,
elegant prince? Whisper what you remember.
What are you thinking, my brother?

The Palais-Royal is filling with ocean.
Salt frosts the golden halls.
Is this your work, O beautiful monster?

Katharine Towers

Nan Hardwicke Turns Into a Hare
(In memory of M)

I will tell you how it was. I slipped
into the hare like a nude foot
into a glorious slipper. Pushing her bones
to one side to make room for my shape
so I could settle like a child within her.
In the dark I groped for her freedom, gently teasing
it apart across my fingers to web across my palm.
Here is where our seperation ends:
I tensed her legs with my arums, pushed my rhythm
down the stepping-stones of spine. An odd feeling this,
to hold another's soul in the mouth like an egg;
the aching jaw around her delicate self. Her mind
was simple, full of open space and weather.
I warmed myself on her frantic pulse and felt the draw
of gorse and grass, the distant slate line
at the edge of the moor. The air span diamonds
out of sea fret to catch across my tawny coat
as I began to fold the earth beneath my feet
and fly across the heath, the heather.

Wendy Pratt

Of Many Worlds in This World

Just like as in a nest of boxes round,
Degrees of sizes in each box are found:
So, in this world, may many others be
Thinner and less, and less still by degree:
Although they are not subject to our sense,
A world may be no bigger than two-pence.
Nature is curious, and such works may shape,
Which our dull senses easily escape:
For creatures, small as atoms, may be there,
If every one a creature's figure bear.
If atoms four, a world can make, then see
What several worlds might in an ear-ring be:
For, millions of those atoms may be in
The head of one small, little, single pin.
And if thus small, then ladies may well wear
A world of worlds, as pendants in each ear.

Margaret Cavendish

Power of the Other

This mind crawls like a pregnant cat; like traffic.
I am in love with the scientists.
They use simple sentence structures. Subject, verb, object.
The sun is a star. Fear is an instinct. The heart is an organ.
Each word is a molecule, the link in a chain, a single step
   along a
winding mountain path – at the end you look back and see a
   brave
new word, a glimmering landscape smiling shyly beneath you.
The scientists are neither charmed nor terrorized.
The scientists are radiant with patience.
They walk calmly, through the woods, through the trees.

Francesca Beard

Friday Afternoon

It was the autumn's last day, when the roof
was skimmed by wings – Red Admiral butterfly? –
a glance of black against the sky, like truth.

It was the day on which the goldfinch flung
its yellow wing against the glass, as though
it had drunk all the sweetness from the sun,

by which, in the wild garden, hips were seen
swelled by last night's rain, crowns under leaves,
as though they could stay glossy, ever green,

a day when children played and did not fall
when traffic stilled to world's edge, a gold crawl,
which I heard, sun-lapped, sleeping through it all.

Alison Brackenbury

Speak of the North!

Speak of the North! A lonely moor
Silent and dark and trackless swells,
The waves of some wild streamlet pour
Hurriedly through its ferny dells.

Profoundly still the twilight air,
Lifeless the landscape; so we deem,
Till like a phantom gliding near
A stag bends down to drink the stream.

And far away a mountain zone,
A cold, white waste of snow-drifts lies,
And one star, large and soft and lone,
Silently lights the unclouded skies.

Charlotte Brontë

A Memory

I remember
The crackle of the palm trees
Over the mooned white roofs of the town . . .
The shining town . . .
And the tender fumbling of the surf
On the sulphur-yellow beaches
As we sat . . . a little apart . . . in the close-pressing night.

The moon hung above us like a golden mango,
And the moist air clung to our faces,
Warm and fragrant as the open mouth of a child
And we watched the out-flung sea
Rolling to the purple edge of the world,
Yet ever back upon itself . . .
As we . . .

Inadequate night . . .
And mooned white memory
Of a tropic sea . . .
How softly it comes up
Like an ungathered lily.

Lola Ridge

Wind and Silver

Greatly shining,
The Autumn moon floats in the thin sky;
And the fish-ponds shake their backs and
   flash their dragon scales
As she passes over them.

Amy Lowell

from The Land

Now in the radiant night no men are stirring:
The little houses sleep with shuttered panes;
Only the hares are wakeful, loosely loping
Along the hedges with their easy gait,
And big loose ears, and pad-prints crossing snow;
The ricks and trees stand silent in the moon,
Loaded with snow, and tiny drifts from branches
Slip to the ground in woods with sliding sigh.
Private the woods, enjoying a secret beauty.

Vita Sackville-West

Twinkled to Sleep

Cerulean night-sky
     Star-set;
Stygian-dark river-plain
East, north, west,
     Dance-set;
Myriad amber-flashing
Lights dancing, rays flashing, all night.

Delight! delight! Inexpressible heart-dance
     With these.
Strange heart-peace, in sparkling lights!
Blithe heart-ease, starry peace, dancing repose!
Star-charmed, dance-enchanted eyes close,
     Appeased.

Dance in jet-dark depth, in star-set height,
Lights dancing, west, east,
Star-high, heart-deep,
     All night.

Ursula Bethell

'I'm glad I exist' – Freedom, Mindfulness and Joy

Reading poetry is a wonderful way to practise mindfulness in a frenetic world. Even the busiest day has space for a poem-sized tea-break or bedtime moment, when we can put aside all distractions and wallow in a few silent minutes of contemplation. Here, poets including Emily Dickinson celebrate the joy of reading and the power it has to sweep us far from humdrum and hectic days. These poets can teach us new ways of looking – as H.D. writes, 'perceiving the other-side of everything' – at the world around us, at happiness and grief, and at ourselves. Their words remind us of the vast and often unexplored territory within us, the solar systems and seascapes of our own imaginations.

One of poetry's greatest pleasures is the discovery that someone, somewhere, at some time, has experienced the same feelings and wrestled with the same anxieties as we have. These poems look within: at tranquillity, or jubilation, or valour. From Winifred Holtby, letting her troubles sink beneath unruffled waters, to Wendy Cope delighted by life's simple enchantments, here are words to savour and shout when life is easy and to hold on to when it isn't.

It Is Everywhere

Green leaves. Wind kissed.
Closed palms. Fresh hope.

Deep river. Free flow.
No signs. Open road.

Wide sky. Grow wings.
Feel light. Dream big.

No frame. New eyes.
From dark. Find light.

Hug air. Laugh loud.
Breathe deep. Dance wild.

Smile wide. Shut eyes.
Hold chest. Close mind.

Ask cloud. Ask wind.
Ask earth. Ask field.

How to   live free?

Hold on. Let Go.
Give trust. Lend heart.

Fall down. Get up.
Eat fear. Drink hope.

Remi Graves

On Foot I Wandered Through the Solar Systems

On foot
I wandered through the solar systems,
before I found the first thread of my red dress.
Already I have a sense of myself.
Somewhere in space my heart hangs,
emitting sparks, shaking the air,
to other immeasurable hearts.

Edith Södergran

Translated by
Malena Mörling and Jonas Ellerström

The Orange

At lunchtime I bought a huge orange –
The size of it made us all laugh.
I peeled it and shared it with Robert and Dave –
They got quarters and I had a half.

And that orange, it made me so happy,
As ordinary things often do
Just lately. The shopping. A walk in the park.
This is peace and contentment. It's new.

The rest of the day was quite easy.
I did all the jobs on my list
And enjoyed them and had some time over.
I love you. I'm glad I exist.

Wendy Cope

New Every Morning

Every day is a fresh beginning,
Listen my soul to the glad refrain.
And, spite of old sorrows
And older sinning,
Troubles forecasted
And possible pain,
Take heart with the day and begin again.

Susan Coolidge

If Once You Have Slept on an Island

If once you have slept on an island
You'll never be quite the same;
You may look as you looked the day before
And go by the same old name,
You may bustle about in street and shop
You may sit at home and sew,
But you'll see blue water and wheeling gulls
Wherever your feet may go.
You may chat with the neighbors of this and that
And close to your fire keep,
But you'll hear ship whistle and lighthouse bell
And tides beat through your sleep.
Oh! you won't know why and you can't say how
Such a change upon you came,
But once you have slept on an island,
You'll never be quite the same.

Rachel Field

Full Moon

She was wearing coral taffeta trousers
Someone had brought her from Isfahan,
And the little gold coat with pomegranate blossoms,
And the coral-hafted feather fan,
But she ran down a Kentish lane in the moonlight,
And skipped in the pool of moon as she ran.

She cared not a rap for all the big planets,
For Betelgeuse or Aldebaran,
And all the big planets cared nothing for her,
That small impertinent charlatan,
But she climbed on a Kentish stile in the moonlight,
And laughed at the sky through the sticks of her fan.

Vita Sackville-West

Seven Times One: Exultation

There's no dew left on the daisies and clover,
    There's no rain left in heaven:
I've said my 'seven times' over and over,
    Seven times one are seven.

I am old, so old, I can write a letter;
    My birthday lessons are done;
The lambs play always, they know no better;
    They are only one times one.

O moon! in the night I have seen you sailing
    And shining so round and low.
You were bright! ah bright! but your light is failing –
    You are nothing now but a bow.

You moon! have you done something wrong in heaven
    That God has hidden your face?
I hope if you have you will soon be forgiven,
    And shine again in your place.

O velvet bee, you're a dusty fellow,
    You've powdered your legs with gold!
O brave marsh marybuds, rich and yellow,
    Give me your money to hold!

O columbine, open your folded wrapper,
  Where two twin turtle-doves dwell!
O cuckoopint, toll me the purple clapper
  That hangs in your clear green bell!

And show me your nest with the young ones in it;
  I will not steal them away;
I am old! you may trust me, linnet, linnet –
  I am seven times one today.

Jean Ingelow

Today

TODAY I will not live up to my potential.
TODAY I will not relate well to my peer group.
TODAY I will not contribute in class.
  I will not volunteer one thing.
TODAY I will not strive to do better.
TODAY I will not achieve or adjust or grow enriched
  or get involved.
I will not put my hand up even if the teacher is wrong
  and I can prove it.

TODAY I might eat the eraser off my pencil.
  I'll look at clouds.
  I'll be late.
  I don't think I'll wash.

I NEED A REST.

Jean Little

Freedom

Give me the long, straight road before me,
    A clear, cold day with a nipping air,
Tall, bare trees to run on beside me,
    A heart that is light and free from care.
Then let me go! – I care not whither
    My feet may lead, for my spirit shall be
Free as the brook that flows to the river,
    Free as the river that flows to the sea.

Olive Runner

To Sleep, Possum to Dream

possum descending a stairwell) a stepladder
numbers of sleep rounded up) possum defending
sealed caves of seal-sheep) sea-clouds) here merely daisies
) telling a petalled profusion of slumbering
possum) enamelled) possum logging out early
possum without compass seeks haystacks in haystacks
thorough innavigable cringly acres
impossumble n 'est pas français a possum's nest
nest pas français a possum cantabile
possum untrainable) the nest unscheduled stop
the nest is silence) the deepest possumism
) opossum knows possum wakes only for possum
so accordingly all possumbilities hold . . .

Vahni Capildeo

Submerged

I have known only my own shallows –
Safe, plumbed places,
Where I was wont to preen myself.
But for the abyss
I wanted a plank beneath
And horizons . . .
I was afraid of the silence
And the slipping toe-hold . . .
Oh, could I now dive
Into the unexplored deeps of me –
Delve and bring up and give
All that is submerged, encased, unfolded,
That is yet the best.

Lola Ridge

The Moon in Your Hands

If you take the moon in your hands
and turn it round
(heavy, slightly tarnished platter)
you're there;

if you pull dry sea-weed from the sand
and turn it round,
and wonder at the underside's bright amber,
your eyes

look out as they did here,
(you don't remember)
when my soul turned round,

perceiving the other-side of everything,
mullein-leaf, dogwood-leaf, moth-wing
and dandelion-seed under the ground.

H.D.

You Who Want

You who want
knowledge,
seek the Oneness
within

There you
will find
the clear mirror
already waiting.

Hadewijch of Antwerp

Boats in the Bay

I will take my trouble and wrap it in a blue handkerchief
And carry it down to the sea.
The sea is as smooth as silk, is as silent as glass;
It does not even whisper
Only the boats, rowed out by the girls in yellow
Ruffle its surface.
It is grey, not blue. It is flecked with boats like midges,
With happy people
Moving soundlessly over the level water.

I will take my trouble and drop it into the water
It is heavy as stone and smooth as a sea-washed pebble.
It will sink under the sea, and the happy people
Will row over it quietly, ruffling the clear water
Little dark boats like midges, skimming silently
Will pass backwards and forwards, the girls singing;
They will never know that they have sailed above sorrow.
Sink heavily and lie still, lie still my trouble.

Winifred Holtby

Three Good Things

At day's end I remember
three good things.

Apples maybe – their skinshine smell
and soft froth of juice.

Water maybe – the pond in the park
dark and full of secret fish.

A mountain maybe – that I saw in a film,
or climbed last holiday,
and suddenly today it thundered up
into a playground game.
Or else an owl – I heard an owl today,
and I made bread.
My head is full of all these things,
it's hard to choose just three.

I let remembering fill me up
with all good things
so that good things will overflow
into my sleeping self,

and in the morning
good things will be waiting
when I wake.

Jan Dean

There Is No Frigate Like a Book

There is no Frigate like a Book
To take us Lands away,
Nor any Coursers like a Page
Of prancing Poetry –
This Travel may the poorest take
Without offence of Toll –
How frugal is the Chariot
That bears the Human soul.

Emily Dickinson

This Poem . . .

This poem is dangerous: it should not be left
Within the reach of children, or even of adults
Who might swallow it whole, with possibly
Undesirable side-effects. If you come across
An unattended, unidentified poem
In a public place, do not attempt to tackle it
Yourself. Send it (preferably, in a sealed container)
To the nearest centre of learning, where it will be rendered
Harmless, by experts. Even the simplest poem
May destroy your immunity to human emotions.
All poems must carry a Government warning. Words
Can seriously affect your heart.

Elma Mitchell

Uppity

Roads around mountains
'cause we can't drive
through

That's Poetry
to Me.

Eileen Myles

Stanzas

Often rebuked, yet always back returning
    To those first feelings that were born with me,
And leaving busy chase of wealth and learning
    For idle dreams of things which cannot be:

Today, I will not seek the shadowy region;
    Its unsustaining vastness waxes drear;
And visions rising, legion after legion,
    Bring the unreal world too strangely near.

I'll walk, but not in old heroic traces,
    And not in paths of high morality,
And not among the half-distinguished faces,
    The clouded forms of long-past history.

I'll walk where my own nature would be leading:
    It vexes me to choose another guide:
Where the grey flocks in ferny glens are feeding;
    Where the wild wind blows on the mountain side.

What have these lonely mountains worth revealing?
    More glory and more grief than I can tell:
The earth that wakes one human heart to feeling
    Can centre both the worlds of Heaven and Hell.

Emily Brontë

Antidote to the Fear of Death

Sometimes as an antidote
To fear of death,
I eat the stars.

Those nights, lying on my back,
I suck them from the quenching dark
Till they are all, all inside me,
Pepper hot and sharp.

Sometimes, instead, I stir myself
Into a universe still young,
Still warm as blood:

No outer space, just space,
The light of all the not yet stars
Drifting like a bright mist,
And all of us, and everything
Already there
But unconstrained by form.

And sometimes it's enough
To lie down here on earth
Beside our long ancestral bones:

To walk across the cobble fields
Of our discarded skulls,
Each like a treasure, like a chrysalis,
Thinking: whatever left these husks
Flew off on bright wings.

Rebecca Elson

'Phenomenal woman' – Society, Fashion and Body Image

Here are poems about navigating society, and the face – and body – we present to the world. Not all of them are sisterly and supportive: bitter rivalry drips from the pens of Dorothy Parker and 'Ephelia'. (The eighteenth century in particular delivered some wonderfully spiteful poetry by men and women alike.) Women have always suffered stricter social constraints than their male counterparts, and here they condemn the straitjacket of decorum and dress. Anna Wickham, writing soon after the heyday of corsets and crinolines, laments the 'trailing gown' that hampers her beloved, and Selina Nwulu's warrior woman edits her wardrobe before battle.

Dora Greenwell beautifully captures the agonies of shyness, and Sylvia Plath probes the fear of ageing in a glossy world that prizes female beauty and youth. Here too, though, are writers rejoicing in themselves, forgiving their imperfect legs in defiance of magazine messaging and embracing wobbling armfuls of remembered pleasure. Cellulite and lightning-bolt stretchmarks don't daunt phenomenal women. Mythical Andromeda is reimagined here, sturdy enough to unchain herself, shrugging off the sea-monster without requiring rescue.

Phenomenal Woman

Pretty women wonder where my secret lies.
I'm not cute or built to suit a fashion model's size
But when I start to tell them,
They think I'm telling lies.
I say,
It's in the reach of my arms,
The span of my hips,
The stride of my step,
The curl of my lips.
I'm a woman
Phenomenally.
Phenomenal woman,
That's me.

I walk into a room
Just as cool as you please,
And to a man,
The fellows stand or
Fall down on their knees.
Then they swarm around me,
A hive of honey bees.
I say,
It's the fire in my eyes,
And the flash of my teeth,
The swing in my waist,
And the joy in my feet.
I'm a woman

Phenomenally.
Phenomenal woman,
That's me.

Men themselves have wondered
What they see in me.
They try so much
But they can't touch
My inner mystery.
When I try to show them,
They say they still can't see.
I say,
It's in the arch of my back,
The sun of my smile,
The ride of my breasts,
The grace of my style.
I'm a woman
Phenomenally.
Phenomenal woman,
That's me.

Now you understand
Just why my head's not bowed.
I don't shout or jump about
Or have to talk real loud.
When you see me passing,
It ought to make you proud.
I say,
It's in the click of my heels,

The bend of my hair,
the palm of my hand,
The need for my care.
'Cause I'm a woman
Phenomenally.
Phenomenal woman,
That's me.

Maya Angelou

Lullaby

Sleep, pretty lady, the night is enfolding you;
   Drift, and so lightly, on crystalline streams
Wrapped in its perfumes, the darkness is holding you;
   Starlight bespangles the way of your dreams.
Chorus the nightingales, wistfully amorous;
   Blessedly quiet, the blare of the day.
All the sweet hours may your visions be glamorous –
   Sleep, pretty lady, as long as you may.

Sleep, pretty lady, the night shall be still for you;
   Silvered and silent, it watches you rest.
Each little breeze, in its eagerness, will for you
   Murmur the melodies ancient and blest.
So in the midnight does happiness capture us;
   Morning is dim with another day's tears.
Give yourself sweetly to images rapturous –
   Sleep, pretty lady, a couple of years.

Sleep, pretty lady, the world awaits day with you;
   Girlish and golden, the slender young moon.
Grant the fond darkness its mystical way with you;
   Morning returns to us ever too soon.
Roses unfold, in their loveliness, all for you;
   Blossom the lilies for hope of your glance.
When you're awake, all the men go and fall for you –
   Sleep, pretty lady, and give me a chance.

Dorothy Parker

To a Proud Beauty

Imperious fool! think not because you're fair,
That you so much above my converse are,
What though the gallants sing your praises loud,
And with false plaudits make you vainly proud?
Though they may tell you all adore your eyes,
And every heart's your willing sacrifice;
Or spin the flatt'ry finer, and persuade
Your easy vanity, that we were made
For foils to make your lustre shine more bright,
And must pay homage to your dazzling light,
Yet know whatever stories they may tell,
All you can boast, is, to be pretty well;
Know too, you stately piece of vanity,
That you are not alone adored, for I
Fantastically might mince, and smile, as well
As you, if airy praise my mind could swell:
Nor are the loud applauses that I have,
For a fine face, or things that Nature gave;
But for acquired parts, a gen'rous mind,
A pleasing converse, neither nice nor kind:
When they that strive to praise you most, can say
No more, but that you're handsome, brisk and gay:
Since then my frame's as great as yours is, why
Should you behold me with a loathing eye?
If you at me cast a disdainful eye,
In biting satire I will rage so high,

Thunder shall pleasant be to what I'll write,
And you shall tremble at my very sight;
Warned by your danger, none shall dare again
Provoke my pen to write in such a strain.

'Ephelia'

A Scherzo: A Shy Person's Wishes

With the wasp at the innermost heart of a peach,
On a sunny wall out of tip-toe reach,
With the trout in the darkest summer pool,
With the fern-seed clinging behind its cool
Smooth frond, in the chink of an aged tree,
In the woodbine's horn with the drunken bee,
With the mouse in its nest in a furrow old,
With the chrysalis wrapped in its gauzy fold;
With things that are hidden, and safe, and bold,
With things that are timid, and shy, and free,
Wishing to be;
With the nut in its shell, with the seed in its pod,
With the corn as it sprouts in the kindly clod,
Far down where the secret of beauty shows
In the bulb of the tulip, before it blows;
With things that are rooted, and firm, and deep,
Quiet to lie, and dreamless to sleep;
With things that are chainless, and tameless, and proud,
With the fire in the jagged thunder-cloud,
With the wind in its sleep, with the wind in its waking,
With the drops that go to the rainbow's making,
Wishing to be with the light leaves shaking,
Or stones in some desolate highway breaking;
Far up on the hills, where no foot surprises
The dew as it falls, or the dust as it rises;

To be couched with the beast in its torrid lair,
Or drifting on ice with the polar bear,
With the weaver at work at his quiet loom;
Anywhere, anywhere, out of this room!

Dora Greenwell

Mirror

I am silver and exact. I have no preconceptions.
Whatever I see I swallow immediately
Just as it is, unmisted by love or dislike.
I am not cruel, only truthful –
The eye of a little god, four-cornered.
Most of the time I meditate on the opposite wall.
It is pink, with speckles. I have looked at it so long
I think it is a part of my heart. But it flickers.
Faces and darkness separate us over and over.

Now I am a lake. A woman bends over me,
Searching my reaches for what she really is.
Then she turns to those liars, the candles or the moon.
I see her back, and reflect it faithfully.
She rewards me with tears and an agitation of hands.
I am important to her. She comes and goes.
Each morning it is her face that replaces the darkness.
In me she has drowned a young girl, and in me an old woman
Rises toward her day after day, like a terrible fish.

Sylvia Plath

A Poet Advises a Change of Clothes

Why wears my lady a trailing gown,
And the spurious gleam of a stage queen's crown?
Let her leap to a horse, and be off to the down!
Astride, let her ride
For the sake of my pride,
That she is more ancient than Diana –
Ancient as that she-ape who, lurking among trees,
Dropt on a grazing zebra, gript him with her knees
And was off across the breadths of the savannah;
Barking her primal merry deviltry,
Barking in forecast of her son's sovereignty.
My timeless lady is as old as she,
And she is moderner moreover
Than Broadway, or an airship, or than Paris lingerie.

O my eternal dominating dear,
How much less dated thou than Guinevere!
Then for your living lover
Change your gown,
And don your queenship when you doff your crown.

Anna Wickham

Tough Dragons

She draws the cliffs of Llanberis and sends it to
the only person who would cry and understand.

It's morning and she can still feel the day in her hands.
The morning she stood up to her father,

she trembled, wearing a scarf from Morocco:
This place is my bones; I don't care if you don't like it.

He said:
*You are fiercely intelligent and when you figure out how
to use them, your words will slay the toughest of dragons.*

She clears her wardrobe, giving away clothes
she doesn't recognize herself in.

Selina Nwulu

Homage to My Hips

these hips are big hips
they need space to
move around in.
they don't fit into little
petty places, these hips
are free hips.
they don't like to be held back.
these hips have never been enslaved,
they go where they want to go
they do what they want to do.
these hips are mighty hips.
these hips are magic hips.
i have known them
to put a spell on a man and
spin him like a top!

Lucille Clifton

My Body

My body is the garden I grew up in,
with tree-trunk legs,
lungs made of rose bushes.
My ribs are a bird cage,
my skin has a sunflower glow.
I have planted vines that wrap up my arms and
around my thighs.
One day I will teach my children to climb them.

My hair is the ocean,
every curl another wave
to hit the shore of my neck,
every freckle a star in the galaxy.
I am constellations.

My shoulders are bird's wings,
my eyes pearls found in a sea of storms.
My stretchmarks are lightning bolts
that show I can survive growth.

Abigail Cook

And then he said: *When did your arms get so big?*

Oh honeybunch, they're not *big*,
they're fat – and every wibbly inch
a rich memory card. This quarter turn
under the left arm, this alabaster,
is the Boston pie last summer,
strident and merciless

and this by my elbow
is the most perfect jam doughnut
I ever had, its sugar curtain
parting, the command performance
stroking my tongue,
its belly dancer middle
jewelled and shadow dancing
with my teeth.

But this here, this favour under my arm
was the perfect cream eclair –
oh my dear, the parting of the slice
and pastry, a thousand naked
wind blown men running bobbly
through the lawns of the National Trust
in Surrey, the ladies in the kitchen
pressing, pressing, into the dough.

Kristina Close

Poem in Which My Legs Are Accepted

Legs!
How we have suffered each other,
never meeting the standards of magazines
or official measurements.

I have hung you from trapezes,
 sat you on wooden rollers,
 pulled and pushed you
 with the anxiety of taffy,
and still, you are yourselves!

Most obvious imperfection, blight on my fantasy life,
strong,
plump,
never to be skinny
or even hinting of the svelte beauties in history books
 or Sears catalogues.
Here you are – solid, fleshy and
white as when I first noticed you, sitting on the toilet,
 spread softly over the wooden seat,
having been with me only twelve years,
 yet
as obvious as the legs of my thirty-year-old gym teacher.

Legs!
O that was the year we did acrobatics in the annual gym show.
How you split for me!
 One-handed cartwheels

from this end of the gymnasium to the other,
ending in double splits,
legs you flashed in blue rayon slacks my mother bought
for the occasion
and tho you were confidently swinging along,
the rest of me blushed at the sound of clapping.

Legs!
How I have worried about you, not able to hide you,
embarrassed at beaches, in highschool
when the cheerleaders' slim brown legs
spread all over
the sand
with the perfection
of bamboo.
I hated you, and still you have never given out on me.

With you
I have risen to the top of blue waves,
with you
I have carried food home as a loving gift
when my arms began
unjelling like madrilene.
Legs, you are a pillow,
white and plentiful with feathers for his wild head.
You are the endless scenery
behind the tense sinewy elegance of his two dark legs.
You welcome him joyfully
and dance.

And you will be the locks in a new canal between continents.
The ship of life will push out of you
and rejoice
in the whiteness,

in the first floating and rising of water.

Kathleen Fraser

Not Andromeda

I cannot hang damselled in the night sky for you
             lunar, the translucent lilt
          of alabaster skin, slender arms,
        fingers which taper to vanishing points
      and, like hot glass, slowly fold into place,
sitting quietly. I cannot grow legs which
slide, waxen, down your glance
with tiny feet bound
to a pulp and my bones
do not quiver with fear
in egg shell threads, stitched together
in diminuendo of the waist and a fine needlework
of the voice.

I cannot be Andromeda.
As a mortal I do not require your worship, nor your
offerings at my feet to guarantee you
a rich harvest. The corners of your plinth bruise
my dappling of cellulite, pomegranate
flesh, clay left
with the impressions of
a creator's thumbs. I possess
a body full and strong, folding like an artery
or a root feasting, sunk in earth – rough, furrowed,
rashed with lichen.

If I am celestial at all, it is because
                    we were both drawn
           from the same flaming blood, a light shed
from the first sighs of the stars.

Let us grasp each other's shoulders.
Let us share a look of understanding.
Let me be a brother to you, even though
I am not a man.

Katie Byford

'But still, like air, I rise' – Courage, Protest and Resistance

Women have always written protest poetry. Female poets campaigned in verse for equality in marriage and in society, fighting with words – and in the case of many of these poets, brave action – against slavery, segregation and sexism among other evils. We cannot assume that the writers of the past would recognize or fully embrace our own beliefs, but for many the act of publishing poetry was a rebellion in itself. It is a woman – Emma Lazarus – whose words grace the Statue of Liberty, and the verses in this section demonstrate the readiness of female writers to defend the downtrodden.

The often ignored contribution of women to the abolition of slavery and the fight for civil rights is here celebrated in the words of extraordinary writers including the freed slave Sojourner Truth and the activist Frances Ellen Watkins Harper. Only a handful of women are generally included in war poetry anthologies, but here are searing verses from Charlotte Mew on the First World War and Colette Bryce on the Troubles in Belfast, among others. There are protests against gender inequality that date back many hundreds of years.

These brave and brilliant words of courage – some serious, a few lighthearted – are wonderful to read and even better learned by heart.

'Hope' is the Thing with Feathers

'Hope' is the thing with feathers –
That perches in the soul –
And sings the tune without the words –
And never stops – at all –

And sweetest – in the Gale – is heard –
And sore must be the storm –
That could abash the little Bird
That kept so many warm –

I've heard it in the chillest land –
And on the strangest Sea –
Yet, never, in Extremity,
It asked a crumb – of Me.

Emily Dickinson

The New Colossus

Not like the brazen giant of Greek fame,
With conquering limbs astride from land to land;
Here at our sea-washed, sunset gates shall stand
A mighty woman with a torch, whose flame
Is the imprisoned lightning, and her name
Mother of Exiles. From her beacon-hand
Glows world-wide welcome; her mild eyes command
The air-bridged harbor that twin cities frame.
'Keep, ancient lands, your storied pomp!' cries she
With silent lips. 'Give me your tired, your poor,
Your huddled masses yearning to breathe free,
The wretched refuse of your teeming shore.
Send these, the homeless, tempest-tost to me,
I lift my lamp beside the golden door!'

Emma Lazarus

Ain't I a Woman?

That man over there say
   a woman needs to be helped into carriages
and lifted over ditches
   and to have the best place everywhere.
Nobody ever helped me into carriages
   or over mud puddles
     or gives me a best place . . .

And ain't I a woman?
   Look at me
Look at my arm!
   I have plowed and planted
and gathered into barns
   and no man could head me . . .
And ain't I a woman?
   I could work as much
and eat as much as a man –
   when I could get to it –
and bear the lash as well
   and ain't I a woman?
I have born thirteen children
   and seen most all sold into slavery
and when I cried out a mother's grief
   none but Jesus heard me . . .
And ain't I a woman?
   that little man in black there say
a woman can't have as much rights as a man

cause Christ wasn't a woman
Where did your Christ come from?
    From God and a woman!
Man had nothing to do with him!
    If the first woman God ever made
was strong enough to turn the world
    upside down, all alone
together women ought to be able to turn it
    rightside up again.

Sojourner Truth

Protest

To sin by silence, when we should protest,
Makes cowards out of men. The human race
Has climbed on protest. Had no voice been raised
Against injustice, ignorance, and lust,
The inquisition yet would serve the law,
And guillotines decide our least disputes.
The few who dare, must speak and speak again
To right the wrongs of many. Speech, thank God,
No vested power in this great day and land
Can gag or throttle. Press and voice may cry
Loud disapproval of existing ills;
May criticize oppression and condemn
The lawlessness of wealth-protecting laws
That let the children and childbearers toil
To purchase ease for idle millionaires.

Therefore I do protest against the boast
Of independence in this mighty land.
Call no chain strong, which holds one rusted link.
Call no land free, that holds one fettered slave.
Until the manacled slim wrists of babes
Are loosed to toss in childish sport and glee,
Until the mother bears no burden, save
The precious one beneath her heart, until
God's soil is rescued from the clutch of greed
And given back to labor, let no man
Call this the land of freedom.

Ella Wheeler Wilcox

Eliza Harris

Like a fawn from the arrow, startled and wild,
A woman swept by us, bearing a child;
In her eye was the night of a settled despair,
And her brow was o'ershaded with anguish and care.

She was nearing the river – in reaching the brink,
She heeded no danger, she paused not to think!
For she is a mother – her child is a slave –
And she'll give him his freedom, or find him a grave!

'Twas a vision to haunt us, that innocent face –
So pale in its aspect, so fair in its grace;
As the tramp of the horse and the bay of the hound,
With the fetters that gall, were trailing the ground!

She was nerved by despair, and strengthen'd by woe,
As she leap'd o'er the chasms that yawn'd from below;
Death howl'd in the tempest, and rav'd in the blast,
But she heard not the sound till the danger was past.

Oh! how shall I speak of my proud country's shame?
Of the stains on her glory, how give them their name?
How say that her banner in mockery waves –
Her 'star-spangled banner' – o'er millions of slaves?

How say that the lawless may torture and chase
A woman whose crime is the hue of her face?
How the depths of forest may echo around
With the shrieks of despair, and the bay of the hound?

With her step on the ice, and her arm on her child,
The danger was fearful, the pathway was wild;
But, aided by Heaven, she gained a free shore,
Where the friends of humanity open'd their door.

So fragile and lovely, so fearfully pale,
Like a lily that bends to the breath of the gale,
Save the heave of her breast, and the sway of her hair,
You'd have thought her a statue of fear and despair.

In agony close to her bosom she press'd
The life of her heart, the child of her breast: –
Oh! love from its tenderness gathering might,
Had strengthen'd her soul for the dangers of flight.

But she's free! – yes, free from the land where the slave
From the hand of oppression must rest in the grave;
Where bondage and torture, where scourges and chains
Have plac'd on our banner indelible stains.

The bloodhounds have miss'd the scent of her way;
The hunter is rifled and foil'd of his prey;
Fierce jargon and cursing, with clanking of chains,
Make sounds of strange discord on Liberty's plains.

With the rapture of love and fullness of bliss,
She plac'd on his brow a mother's fond kiss: –
Oh! poverty, danger and death she can brave,
For the child of her love is no longer a slave!

Frances Ellen Watkins Harper

Rosa Parks

she sorts the drawer
knives at the left
forks at the right
spoons in the middle
like neat silver petals
curved inside each other

the queue sorts itself
snaking through the bus
whites at the front
blacks at the back

but people are not knives
not forks
not spoons
their bones are full of stardust
their hearts full of songs
and the sorting on the bus
is just plain wrong

so Rosa says no
and Rosa won't go
to the place for her race

she'll face up to all the fuss
but she's said goodbye
to the back of the bus

Jan Dean

My First Day at School

I remember . . .
Momma scrubbed my face, hard.
Plaited my hair, tight.
Perched a hopeful white bow on my head,
Like a butterfly hoping for flight.

She shone my shoes, black, shiny, neat.
Another hopeful bow, on each toe,
To give wings to my feet.

My dress was standing to attention, stiff with starch.
My little battledress.
And now, my march.

Two marshals march in front of me.
Two marshals march behind of me.
The people scream and jeer at me.
Their faces are red, not white.

The marshals tower above me, a grey-legged wall.
Broad of back, white of face and tall, tall, tall.
I only see their legs and shoes as black and shiny as mine.
They march along, stern and strong. I try to march in time.

One hisses to another, 'Slow down it ain't a race.
She only take little bitty girlie steps.'
I quicken my pace.

Head up.
Eyes straight.
I march into school.
To learn like any other kid can.

And maybe to teach a lesson too.

Michaela Morgan

Wanted: A Husband

Wanted a husband who doesn't suppose,
That all earthly employments one feminine knows, –
That she'll scrub, do the cleaning, and cooking, and baking,
And plain needlework, hats and caps, and dressmaking.
Do the family washing, yet always look neat,
Mind the bairns, with a temper unchangeably sweet,
Be a cheerful companion, whenever desired,
And contentedly toil day and night, if required.
Men expecting as much, one may easily see,
But they're not what is wanted, at least, not by me.

Marion Bernstein

To the Ladies

Wife and servant are the same,
But only differ in the name:
For when that fatal knot is tied,
Which nothing, nothing can divide,
When she the word *Obey* has said,
And man by law supreme has made,
Then all that's kind is laid aside,
And nothing left but state and pride.
Fierce as an eastern prince he grows,
And all his innate rigour shows:
Then but to look, to laugh, or speak,
Will the nuptial contract break.
Like mutes she signs alone must make,
And never any freedom take,
But still be governed by a nod,
And fear her husband as a god:
Him still must serve, him still obey,
And nothing act, and nothing say,
But what her haughty lord thinks fit,
Who with the power, has all the wit.
Then shun, oh! shun that wretched state,
And all the fawning flatt'rers hate:
Value your selves, and men despise,
You must be proud, if you'll be wise.

Lady Mary Chudleigh

The Battle of the Sexes

Bobby Riggs, tennis champ,
said a woman couldn't
beat a man . . .

Billie Jean King, tennis champ,
in three straight sets, showed
a woman can.

Liz Brownlee

Still I Rise

You may write me down in history
With your bitter, twisted lies,
You may trod me in the very dirt
But still, like dust, I'll rise.

Does my sassiness upset you?
Why are you beset with gloom?
'Cause I walk like I've got oil wells
Pumping in my living room.

Just like moons and like suns,
With the certainty of tides,
Just like hopes springing high,
Still I'll rise.

Did you want to see me broken?
Bowed head and lowered eyes?
Shoulders falling down like teardrops,
Weakened by my soulful cries?

Does my haughtiness offend you?
Don't you take it awful hard
'Cause I laugh like I've got gold mines
Diggin' in my own backyard.

You may shoot me with your words,
You may cut me with your eyes,
You may kill me with your hatefulness,
But still, like air, I'll rise.

Does my sexiness upset you?
Does it come as a surprise
That I dance like I've got diamonds
At the meeting of my thighs?

Out of the huts of history's shame
I rise
Up from a past that's rooted in pain
I rise
I'm a black ocean, leaping and wide,
Welling and swelling I bear in the tide.

Leaving behind nights of terror and fear
I rise
Into a daybreak that's wondrously clear
I rise
Bringing the gifts that my ancestors gave,
I am the dream and the hope of the slave.
I rise
I rise
I rise.

Maya Angelou

Saltwater

Everyone who terrifies you is 65 per cent water.
And everyone you love is made of stardust,
and I know
sometimes
you cannot breathe deeply, and
the night sky is no home, and
that you are down to your last 2 per cent,
but
nothing is infinite,
not even loss.
You are made of the sea and the stars, and
one day,
you are going to find yourself again.

Finn Butler

The Call

From our low seat beside the fire
  Where we have dozed and dreamed and watched the glow
  Or raked the ashes, stopping so
We scarcely saw the sun or rain
  Above, or looked much higher
Than this same quiet red or burned-out fire.
      To-night we heard a call,
      A rattle on the window-pane,
      A voice on the sharp air,
And felt a breath stirring our hair,
  A flame within us: Something swift and tall
  Swept in and out and that was all.
Was it a bright or a dark angel? Who can know?
  It left no mark upon the snow,
    But suddenly it snapped the chain
    Unbarred, flung wide the door
    Which will not shut again;
  And so we cannot sit here any more.

      We must arise and go:
    The world is cold without
    And dark and hedged about
  With mystery and enmity and doubt,
     But we must go
     Though yet we do not know
Who called, or what marks we shall leave upon the snow.

Charlotte Mew

Before I Leave the Stage

Before I leave the stage
I will sing the only song
I was meant truly to sing.

It is the song
of I AM.
Yes: I am Me
&
You.
WE ARE.

I love Us with every drop
of our blood
every atom of our cells
our waving particles
– undaunted flags of our Being –
neither here nor there.

Alice Walker

The Juniper Tree

See that lovely juniper, pressed so hard,
angry winds swirl round her, but she'll not let
her leaves fall or scatter; clenched, branches held
high, she gathers strength; her refuge within.

This, my friend, is a picture of my soul
standing firm against all; if life's ravaged,
weakened me, my fear's contained, and I win
by enduring a pain which makes it hurt

to breathe. Mine was a noble dream, sheltered
in his splendour and love, my pride would be
restored; I would encounter life's bitter

battles. Nature taught this tree to resist:
in me you see what reason can perform
how from the worst evil good can grow.

Vittoria Colonna

Ruth

Brown girl chanting Te Deums on Sunday
Rust-colored peasant with strength of granite,
Bronze girl welding ship hulls on Monday,
Let nothing smirch you, let no one crush you.

Queen of ghetto, sturdy hill-climber,
Walk with the lilt of ballet dancer,
Walk like a strong down-East wind blowing,
Walk with the majesty of the First Woman.

Gallant challenger, millioned-hope bearer,
The stars are your beacons, earth your inheritance,
Meet blaze and cannon with your own heart's passion,
Surrender to none the fire of your soul.

Pauli Murray

Inventory

Four be the things I am wiser to know:
Idleness, sorrow, a friend, and a foe.

Four be the things I'd been better without:
Love, curiosity, freckles, and doubt.

Three be the things I shall never attain:
Envy, content, and sufficient champagne.

Three be the things I shall have till I die:
Laughter and hope and a sock in the eye.

Dorothy Parker

93 Percent Stardust

We have calcium in our bones,
iron in our veins,
carbon in our souls,
and nitrogen in our brains.
93 percent stardust,
with souls made of flames,
we are all just stars
that have people names.

Nikita Gill

God Says Yes To Me

I asked God if it was okay to be melodramatic
and she said yes
I asked her if it was okay to be short
and she said it sure is
I asked her if I could wear nail polish
or not wear nail polish
and she said honey
she calls me that sometimes
she said you can do just exactly
what you want to
Thanks God I said
And is it even okay if I don't paragraph
my letters
Sweetcakes God said
who knows where she picked that up
what I'm telling you is
Yes Yes Yes

Kaylin Haught

Warning

When I am an old woman I shall wear purple
With a red hat which doesn't go, and doesn't suit me.
And I shall spend my pension on brandy and summer gloves
And satin sandals, and say we've no money for butter.
I shall sit down on the pavement when I'm tired
And gobble up samples in shops and press alarm bells
And run my stick along the public railings
And make up for the sobriety of my youth.
I shall go out in my slippers in the rain
And pick the flowers in other people's gardens
And learn to spit.

You can wear terrible shirts and grow more fat
And eat three pounds of sausages at a go
Or only bread and pickle for a week
And hoard pens and pencils and beermats and things in
    boxes.

But now we must have clothes that keep us dry
And pay our rent and not swear in the street
And set a good example for the children.
We must have friends to dinner and read the papers.

But maybe I ought to practise a little now?
So people who know me are not too shocked and surprised
When suddenly I am old, and start to wear purple.

Jenny Joseph

May 1915

Let us remember Spring will come again
    To the scorched, blackened woods, where the
      wounded trees
    Wait, with their old wise patience for the heavenly rain,
Sure of the sky: sure of the sea to send its healing breeze,
    Sure of the sun. And even as to these
      Surely the Spring, when God shall please
    Will come again like a divine surprise
To those who sit to-day with their great Dead, hands in their
    hands, eyes in their eyes,
At one with Love, at one with Grief: blind to the scattered
    things and changing skies.

Charlotte Mew

Immensity

You go at night into immensity,
Leaving this green earth, where hawthorn flings
Pale stars on hedgerows, and our serenity
Is twisted into strange shapes; my heart never sings
Now on spring mornings, for you fly at nightfall
From this earth I know
Toward the clear stars, and over all
Those dark seas and waiting towns you go;
And when you come to me
There are fearful dreams in your eyes,
And remoteness. Oh, God! I see
How far away you are,
Who may so soon meet death beneath an alien star.

Mabel Esther Allan

The Brits

Whatever it was they were looking for, they liked
to arrive in the small hours, take us by surprise,
avoiding our eyes like gormless youngfellas
shuffling at a dance. My mother spoke:
a nod from the leader and the batch of heavy rifles
was stacked, *clackety-clack*, like a neat camp fire
under the arch of the hall table – her one
condition, with so many children
in their beds – each gun placed by a soldier
whose face, for an instant, hung in the mirror.
This doe, the load of them thundered up the stairs,
filling our rooms like news of a tragedy.

Last night I dreamt of tiny soldiers
like the action figures I played with as a child;
Fay Wray soldiers in the clumsy hands of Kong,
little Hasbro troopers in the massive hands of God.
I'd like to remove their camouflage and radios,
to dress them up in doll-sized clothes; little high street shirts,
jeans, trainers, the strip of ordinary sons and brothers.
I'd like to hand them back to their mothers.

Colette Bryce

There Will Come Soft Rains

There will come soft rains and the smell of the
    ground,
And swallows circling with their shimmering
    sound;

And frogs in the pools, singing at night,
And wild plum trees in tremulous white,

Robins will wear their feathery fire,
Whistling their whims on a low fence-wire;

And not one will know of the war, not one
Will care at last when it is done.

Not one would mind, neither bird nor tree,
If mankind perished utterly;

And Spring herself, when she woke at dawn,
Would scarcely know that we were gone.

Sara Teasdale

'Behind Me – dips Eternity' – Endings

We reach for poetry at funerals, as at weddings, because it can say things we can't. Death was once a familiar, family business that happened in the home, as here in Joanna Baillie's domestic drama. It must always have been particularly present to women, most of whom would face the then perilous experience of childbirth. It is no wonder, then, that the Victorians, especially, embraced a cult of sentimental morbidity and wrote so much on the subject. It has even been suggested that Victorian women – many of them idle not by choice but because they were deprived of education and stimulating employment, cloistered at home – naturally fell to brooding and dark thoughts. Whenever they lived, however, poets have always been drawn to this great and final subject. Here are words of deep and beautiful sadness, but also lines to bring comfort and hope.

Remember

Remember me when I am gone away,
    Gone far away into the silent land;
    When you can no more hold me by the hand,
Nor I half turn to go yet turning stay.
Remember me when no more day by day
    You tell me of our future that you planned:
    Only remember me; you understand
It will be late to counsel then or pray.
Yet if you should forget me for a while
    And afterwards remember, do not grieve:
    For if the darkness and corruption leave
    A vestige of the thoughts that once I had,
Better by far you should forget and smile
    Than that you should remember and be sad.

Christina Rossetti

Not Waving but Drowning

Nobody heard him, the dead man,
But still he lay moaning:
I was much further out than you thought
And not waving but drowning.

Poor chap, he always loved larking
And now he's dead
It must have been too cold for him his heart gave way,
They said.

Oh, no no no, it was too cold always
(Still the dead one lay moaning)
I was much too far out all my life
And not waving but drowning.

Stevie Smith

The Child in Me

She follows me about my House of Life
(This happy little ghost of my dead youth!)
She has no part in Time's relentless strife
She keeps her old simplicity and truth –
And laughs at grim mortality,
This deathless child that stays with me –
This happy little ghost of my dead youth!

My House of Life is weather-stained with years –
(O Child in Me, I wonder why you stay.)
Its windows are bedimmed with rain of tears,
The walls have lost their rose, its thatch is gray.
One after one its guests depart,
So dull a host is my old heart.
O Child in Me, I wonder why *You* stay!

For jealous Age, whose face I would forget,
Pulls the bright flowers you bring me from my hair
And powders it with snow; and yet – and yet
I love your dancing feet and jocund air.
I have no taste for caps of lace
To tie about my faded face –
I love to wear *your* flower in my hair.

O Child in Me, leave not my House of Clay
Until we pass together through its door!
When lights are out, and Life has gone away
And we depart to come again no more.
We comrades who have travelled far
Will hail the Twilight and the Star,
And smiling, pass together through the Door!

May Riley Smith

September Rain

Always rain, September rain,
The slipstream of the season,
Night of the equinox, the change.

There are three surfers out back.
Now the rain's pulse is doubled, the wave
Is not to be caught. Are they lost in the dark

Do they know where the coast is combed with light
Or is there only the swell, lifting
Back to the beginning

When they ran down the hill like children
Through this rain, September rain,
And the sea opened its breast to them?

I lie and listen
And the life in me stirs like a tide
That knows when it must be gone.

I am on the deep deep water
Lightly held by one ankle
Out of my depth, waiting.

Helen Dunmore

Woodland Burial

Don't lay me in some gloomy churchyard shaded by a wall
Where the dust of ancient bones has spread a dryness over
   all,
Lay me in some leafy loam where, sheltered from the cold
Little seeds investigate and tender leaves unfold.
There kindly and affectionately, plant a native tree
To grow resplendent before God and hold some part of me.
The roots will not disturb me as they wend their peaceful way
To build the fine and bountiful, from closure and decay.
To seek their small requirements so that when their work is
   done
I'll be tall and standing strongly in the beauty of the sun.

Pam Ayres

The Things That Matter

Now that I've nearly done my days,
And grown too stiff to sweep or sew,
I sit and think, till I'm amaze,
About what lots of things I know:
Things as I've found out one by one –
And when I'm fast down in the clay,
My knowing things and how they're done
Will all be lost and thrown away.

There's things, I know, as won't be lost,
Things as folks write and talk about:
The way to keep your roots from frost,
And how to get your ink spots out.
What medicine's good for sores and sprains,
What way to salt your butter down,
What charms will cure your different pains,
And what will bright your faded gown.

But more important things than these,
They can't be written in a book:
How fast to boil your greens and peas,
And how good bacon ought to look;
The feel of real good wearing stuff,
The kind of apple as will keep,
The look of bread that's rose enough,
And how to get a child asleep.

Whether the jam is fit to pot,
Whether the milk is going to turn,
Whether a hen will lay or not,
Is things as some folks never learn.
I know the weather by the sky,
I know what herbs grow in what lane;
And if sick men are going to die,
Or if they'll get about again.

Young wives come in, a-smiling, grave,
With secrets that they itch to tell:
I know what sort of times they'll have,
And if they'll have a boy or gell.
And if a lad is ill to bind,
Or some young maid is hard to lead,
I know when you should speak 'em kind,
And when it's scolding as they need.

I used to know where birds ud set,
And likely spots for trout or hare,
And God may want me to forget
The way to set a line or snare;
But not the way to truss a chick,
To fry a fish, or baste a roast,
Nor how to tell, when folks are sick,
What kind of herb will ease them most!

Forgetting seems such silly waste!
I know so many little things,
And now the Angels will make haste
To dust it all away with wings!
O God, you made me like to know,
You kept the things straight in my head,
Please God, if you can make it so,
Let me know something when I'm dead.

Edith Nesbit

Behind Me – dips Eternity

Behind Me – dips Eternity –
Before Me – Immortality –
Myself – the Term between –
Death but the Drift of Eastern Gray,
Dissolving into Dawn away,
Before the West begin –

'Tis Kingdoms – afterward – they say –
In perfect – pauseless Monarchy –
Whose Prince – is Son of None –
Himself – His Dateless Dynasty –
Himself – Himself diversify –
In Duplicate divine –

'Tis Miracle before Me – then –
'Tis Miracle behind – between –
A Crescent in the Sea –
With Midnight to the North of Her –
And Midnight to the South of Her –
And Maelstrom – in the Sky –

Emily Dickinson

About the Poets

Fleur Adcock (born 1934)

Fleur moved from her native New Zealand to England during the Second World War, returning to settle in London in 1963. She has been writing since she was five, working as a librarian before becoming a full-time writer. Fleur has published ten poetry collections as well as a collected edition, and often gives voice to the powerless in her work. She was awarded an OBE in 1996.

Kissing is on page 82.

Mabel Esther Allan (1915–1998)

Although her terrible eyesight meant she hated school, Mabel decided at the age of eight that she wanted to be a writer, and her supportive father bought her a desk and taught her to type. Her first book was published in 1945 and she went on to write about 170 children's books, including the 'Drina' series of ballet stories. During the Second World War she served in the Women's Land Army in Cheshire and taught in a school for deprived children in Liverpool. Four of her books were set during war-time. She also published under the names Jean Estoril, Priscilla Hagon and Anne Pilgrim.

Immensity is on page 201.

Deborah Alma (born 1964)

Deborah has worked with people with dementia and with vulnerable women's groups. She is editor of *Emergency Poet: An Anti-Stress Poetry Anthology*, *The Everyday Poet: Poems to Live By* and the award-winning *#MeToo: A Women's Poetry Anthology*. Her *True Tales of the Countryside* is published by the Emma Press and her first full collection

Dirty Laundry is from Nine Arches Press.
I Am My Own Parent is on page 18.

Astrid Hjertenæs Andersen (1915–1985)

Astrid was a Norwegian poet and travel writer who worked as a journalist for Norway's biggest newspaper. She married the painter Snorre Andersen and they often worked together: he would illustrate her poetry and she wrote poems inspired by his nature paintings. She published numerous collections of poetry and won many prizes in Norway, including the prestigious Norwegian Critics Prize for Literature in 1964.

Before the sun goes down is on page 69.

Maya Angelou (1928–2014)

Maya was born in St Louis, Missouri. She was attacked by her mother's boyfriend as a child, and he was killed by her uncles. Maya refused to speak for five years after that, but did develop a deep passion for reading. After school, she had various jobs including being a streetcar conductor and stripping paint from cars, eventually making a name for herself as a nightclub singer. The first of her several autobiographies, *I Know Why the Caged Bird Sings*, told her story up until the age of seventeen, when her son was born, and it was – and remains – hugely popular. From the 1950s she worked in the civil rights movement with Martin Luther King Jr and Malcolm X. Maya was also an award-winning actress and the first black woman to have a screenplay produced. Her fabulous performances – including reading 'On The Pulse of Morning' at the inauguration of President Bill Clinton – are legendary.

Phenomenal Woman / Still I Rise are on pages 152 and 189.

Margaret Atwood (born 1939)

Margaret is the author of more than fifty books of fiction, poetry and critical essays. Her recent novels are *The Heart Goes Last* and the MaddAddam Trilogy – the Giller and Booker Prize-shortlisted *Oryx and Crake*, *The Year of the Flood* and *MaddAddam*. Other novels include *The Blind Assassin*, winner of the Booker Prize, *Alias Grace*, *The Robber Bride*, *Cat's Eye*, *The Penelopiad* (a retelling of the Odyssey) and the modern classic *The Handmaid's Tale* – now a critically acclaimed television series. *Hag-Seed*, a novel based on Shakespeare's play *The Tempest*, was published in 2016. Her most recent graphic series is *Angel Catbird*. In 2017, she was awarded the German Peace Prize, the Franz Kafka International Literary Prize, and the PEN Center USA Lifetime Achievement Award.

Siren Song is on page 61.

Ruth Awolola (born 1998)

Ruth is a British born Nigerian Jamaican student, youth worker, sister, daughter, friend and poet. She grew up in South East London but is currently based in York where she studies English in Education. She has been performing poetry since 2015 and has performed up and down the UK, exploring themes of travelling, race, family and space. In 2018, *Rising Stars*, an anthology of poetry from new poets including Ruth, was Highly Commended at the CLiPPA ceremony.

On Forgetting That I Am A Tree is on page 30.

Pam Ayres (born 1947)

Pam recited one of her poems on local radio in 1974 and her friends badgered her to enter a television talent show in the following year. Both paved the way for her to become a much-loved performer and broadcaster who has sold millions of books, CDs and DVDs, toured internationally and been studied in schools around the world. Her books have often topped lists of the 'most borrowed' from libraries and she was awarded an MBE in 2004.

Woodland Burial is on page 211.

Francesca Beard (born 1968)

Francesca was born in Malaysia and lives in London. A leading performance poet, her shows have been called 'spine-tingling' (the *Independent*). She has had dramas performed at the Royal Court Theatre and on BBC Radio 4 and has been Poet in Residence at venues including the Tower of London, the Natural History Museum and the Metropolitan Police. Francesca tours schools, theatres and festivals with shows and workshops and has performed around the world.

Power of the Other is on page 119.

Marion Bernstein (1846–1906)

Marion was a radical feminist poet in Victorian Glasgow. She was ill throughout her life and had to apply for charitable grants when she was too unwell to give piano lessons. She kept in touch with the world through newspapers when she was bedridden, and wrote poems inspired by the subjects they covered, including politics, domestic violence, slavery and working-class poverty. Many were published in periodicals, and one book of poetry was published in 1876. Marion had been largely forgotten until the 1990s but in 2013 her collected poems – including previously unseen work – was finally published as *A Song of Glasgow Town*.

Wanted: A Husband is on page 186.

Liz Berry (born 1980)

Liz was born and raised in the Black Country and the language and folklore of the region is a huge influence on her poetry – she loves to scour old dictionaries for dialect words to rescue and use. She worked as a primary school teacher and wrote poetry in secret until her twenties, when she studied for a Masters degree and began to publish her work. Her collection *Black Country* won the Forward Prize for Best First Collection, among other awards, in 2014.

5th Dudley Girl Guides is on page 34.

Ursula Bethell (1874–1945)

Ursula was born in Surrey, England, but her family moved to New Zealand while she was a baby. Her father was a prosperous sheep farmer and she was given an expensive international education, studying painting and music in Europe. She eventually settled back in New Zealand and undertook charity and social work. She lived with Effie Pollen. Ursula only started to write poetry aged around fifty, and stopped when Effie died, so all her work is from one decade between 1924 and 1934. She was a talented garden designer and many of her poems were inspired by gardening. She originally published under the pseudonym 'Evelyn Hayes' – apparently a great-great-grandfather of Ursula's who had been deported to Botany Bay for kidnapping an heiress.

Twinkled to Sleep is on page 125.

Hera Lindsay Bird (born 1987)

Hera is from Wellington, New Zealand, where she works in a bookshop. Her first book, *Hera Lindsay Bird*, was published in 2016, and her second, *Pamper Me to Hell and Back*, in 2018. Some of her poems – including 'Monica', about the *Friends* character – have been viral online sensations. Her caustic, witty verses have won her many awards and legions of fans. She likes murder mysteries and watching ice-skating.

Love Comes Back is on page 88.

Elizabeth Bishop (1911–1979)

Elizabeth's father died when she was a baby, and her mother was committed to a psychiatric hospital not long afterwards, so she was brought up by her grandparents. She intended to become a doctor until she met the poet Marianne Moore at Vassar College – Marianne became a lifelong friend and inspired Elizabeth to embark on a writing career instead. She didn't write many poems – only 101 were published during her lifetime – but worked tirelessly on each one, polishing it to perfection. Elizabeth lived in Brazil with her partner, the architect Lota de Macedo Soares, for fourteen years, before Lota's tragic suicide.
One Art is on page 92.

Louise Bogan (1897–1970)

Louise had a difficult childhood: her unstable mother indulged in public love affairs and mysterious disappearances, and the family moved around a lot. Her family wasn't wealthy, but a kindly benefactor funded her studies when she showed promise at school. She lived most of her life in New York, where she was friends with writers including William Carlos Williams, and was poetry editor of the *New Yorker* magazine for four decades. Louise had a daughter with her first husband, but struggled with poverty and depression when they later separated. Her poems were greatly praised during her lifetime, and she was the fourth Poet Laureate to the Library of Congress in 1945.
Song for the Last Act is on page 80.

Aisha Borja

Aisha comes from the Colombia of her father's family. Despite struggling with profound dyslexia, she has won both the Foyle Competition and the First Story National Writers Award for her work.
Bridge is on page 16.

Alison Brackenbury (born 1953)

Alison grew up in Lincolnshire. Her latest book, *Aunt Margaret's Pudding* (HappenStance Press, 2018), celebrates the strength, humour and cooking of Dot, her indomitable country grandmother. Her next book will be her *Selected Poems* (Carcanet, February 2019). This celebrates the fact that Alison, now a town-dweller, has done far less cooking than Dot – and almost no ironing.
Friday Afternoon is on page 120.

Anne Bradstreet (c. 1612–1672)

Though sometimes known as America's first poet, Anne grew up in Northamptonshire, where her father worked for the Earl of Lincoln. As a child she was a 'devourer of books' in the Earl's library. Her family emigrated to the newly settled American colonies, where Anne and her husband – later Governor of Salem during the famous witch trials – had eight children. Although she also wrote about other subjects, Anne's writing about her family is her best loved today. It was rather scandalous for a woman to publish at that time. Her brother-in-law printed her work without her knowledge back in London, and early editions took great pains to emphasize her respectability.
To My Dear and Loving Husband is on page 76.

Anne Brontë (1820–1849)

Anne's novel *Agnes Grey* was inspired by her time as a governess. Its heroine was a petted and patronized youngest sibling who grew up among rugged hills – so we can draw our own conclusions about Brontë family dynamics from that! She had to leave her post after persuading her employers to hire her feckless brother Branwell, who embarked on an affair with the lady of the house. She and her elder sisters Charlotte and Emily published their poetry under male pseudonyms as

Acton, Currer and Ellis Bell. Disappointed by pitiful sales of two copies in a year, they worked intensively on their novels instead, pacing the dining room and critiquing each other's work. Anne's novel *The Tenant of Wildfell Hall* – in which a woman flees her cruel, alcoholic husband – was considered shocking but was a huge hit. Anne died from tuberculosis aged only twenty-nine.

Lines Composed in a Wood on a Windy Day is on page 102.

Charlotte Brontë (1816–1855)

After a sheltered childhood on the Yorkshire moors, Charlotte travelled to Brussels with her sister Emily to learn French. There, she fell miserably in love with the married owner of their boarding house – a passion that inspired her novels *Villette* and *The Professor*. *Jane Eyre* was published in 1847 and was an immediate bestseller. She survived her siblings and married, though slightly unenthusiastically. She died in 1855.

Speak of the North! is on page 121.

Emily Brontë (1818–1848)

Many of Emily's poems originated in her gothic-flavoured writings about Gondal, an imaginary island realm created with her sister, Anne. Emily's masterpiece *Wuthering Heights* was, like much of her poetry, inspired by the wild beauty of the Yorkshire moors where the sisters lived with their father and brother. She died from tuberculosis aged only thirty.

High Waving Heather / Stanzas are on pages 99 and 147.

Elizabeth Barrett Browning (1806–1861)

Elizabeth received an excellent education at home from her adoring but overprotective father, and published poetry from her teens onwards. Despite living as an invalid and recluse – perhaps devastated at her brother drowning, perhaps injured in a fall from a horse – her poetry was hugely popular. She attracted fan mail from Robert Browning – then an aspiring poet, six years her junior – and their relationship revived her sufficiently to elope with him to Italy, get married and have a son. Her father never forgave them. A greater celebrity than her husband during their lifetimes, Elizabeth also involved herself in contemporary politics. She was a passionate critic of slavery and child labour, and her epic poem *Aurora Leigh* was remarkable for its strong heroine and contemporary setting.

Sonnet 43 / Extract from Aurora Leigh are on pages 70 and 109.

Liz Brownlee (born 1958)

Liz went to nine different schools before she was eleven. She wrote and drew as a child and began again when her own children were small. She gives workshops at schools, libraries and festivals on the subjects of her books: endangered animals, extraordinary women, empathy, and shape poems. Liz goes everywhere accompanied by her assistance dog, miniature labradoodle Lola.

Battle of the Sexes is on page 188.

Colette Bryce (born 1970)

Colette is an award-winning poet from Northern Ireland. Born and brought up in Derry, she moved to England as a student in 1988 and settled in London for some years while starting out as a writer. She received the Eric Gregory Award for emerging poets in 1995. After a year teaching in Madrid, she took up a fellowship at Dundee University from 2002 to 2005, and was subsequently appointed North East Literary Fellow at the universities of Newcastle and Durham. She currently lives in Newcastle-upon-Tyne, where she works as a freelance writer and editor.

The Brits is on page 202.

Helen Burke (born 1953)

Helen was born in Doncaster to Irish parents and started writing poetry in 1989. Her poems have been widely published and anthologized, and she has won numerous prizes. Since the 1970s, Helen's poems have appeared in pamphlets, on greetings cards, on pieces of origami, on radio, on tape, on CD, on the side of stray dogs and in a million other places. Her verses have been set to music by an Australian orchestra and she has performed with jazz, rock and Irish folk musicians.
Lacing Boots is on page 36.

Finn Butler

Originally from London, Finn now lives and works in Japan. Her first poetry collection, *From The Wreckage*, was published in 2014. She holds a degree in music from Goldsmiths and released an EP, *We Are Laughing*, in 2017. Her work is inspired by meditation and time spent in nature, though she can also be found arguing the feminist cause over a pint at her local pub. She is currently working on a novel, to be dedicated to her primary school teacher in fulfilment of a long-held promise.
Saltwater is on page 191.

Katie Byford

Katie wrote a prize-winning university dissertation about the poet Sappho and has worked in poetry, photography, writing, graphic design and film with organizations including the Wellcome Collection, Horniman Museum and London South Bank University. She has been a member of Barbican Young Poets and gives talks and workshops on classical subjects and poetry.
Not Andromeda is on page 169.

Moya Cannon (born 1965)

Moya was born in County Donegal and now lives in Dublin. She has taught in various schools and universities, been writer in residence at Trent University Ontario and Kerry County Council, and edited *Poetry Ireland* in 1995. She has collaborated with musicians including traditional Irish singers and a string quartet, and a bilingual Spanish/English edition of her poems was published in Spain in 2015, translated by the respected Argentinian poet Jorge Fondebrider.
Introductions is on page 50.

Vahni Capildeo (born 1973)

Scottish/Trinidadian poet Vahni have lived in the UK since 1991. They read Old Norse and translation theory at Oxford. Their published books of poetry include *Measures of Expatriation* (2016), which won the Forward Prize for Best Collection. They have worked at the Oxford English Dictionary, for Commonwealth Writers, and in academia. They are the Douglas Caster Cultural Fellow in Poetry at the University of Leeds.
To Sleep Possum to Dream is on page 138.

Margaret Cavendish, Duchess of Newcastle (c. 1623–1674)

Happily married to William Cavendish, a poet and Cavalier commander during the English Civil War, Margaret's aristocratic background enabled her to write in an age when a woman selling books was considered shocking. An eccentric celebrity – children would follow her carriage through London to catch a glimpse of her. She wrote many books including plays, fiction, science and philosophy, and was among the first women invited to visit the scientific Royal Society. She often criticized the restrictions imposed on women at that time in her writing.
Of Many Worlds in This World is on page 118.

Mary Jean Chan

Born and raised in Hong Kong, Mary Jean currently lives and works in London. She is the author of the pamphlet *A Hurry of English* (Poetry Book Society Summer Pamphlet Choice) and her debut poetry collection is forthcoming from Faber & Faber (July 2019). She came second in the 2017 National Poetry Competition, and was shortlisted for the 2017 Forward Prize for Best Single Poem. Mary Jean is currently a PhD candidate and Research Associate in Creative Writing at Royal Holloway, the University of London, and is an editor of *Oxford Poetry*. *Practice* is on page 59.

Lady Mary Chudleigh (1656–1710)

Born into an upper-class Devon family, Mary married the third Baronet of Ashton. It's unclear how happy they were, as she does write rather a lot about marriage being a prison – but she did publish fiercely feminist poetry and essays at a time when many husbands would have prevented her. Mary argued for women's rights and education and the reform of the oppressive marriage laws, as well as praising female friendship. She had at least six children.
To the Ladies is on page 187.

Kate Clanchy (born 1965)

Kate was born and grew up in Scotland but now lives in Oxford. Her poetry collections *Slattern*, *Samarkand* and *Newborn* have brought her many literary awards and a wide audience. She is the author of the much acclaimed *Antigona and Me*, and was the 2009 winner of the BBC Short Story Award. She has also written extensively for Radio 4. Her first novel, *Meeting the English*, was published by Picador in 2013 and was shortlisted for the 2013 Costa First Book Award and longlisted for the 2014 Desmond Elliott Prize. Her first collection of stories, *The Not-Dead and the Saved*, was published by Picador in June 2015. Kate's anthology of poems from the students of Oxford Spires Academy, *England: Poems from a School*, was published in June 2018 by Picador.

Timetable is on page 11.

Polly Clark (born 1968)

Polly has had various jobs including zoo-keeping and teaching English in Hungary. Her poetry has won many prizes, and she was selected as one of *Mslexia* magazine's ten best poets of the decade in 2014. Her debut novel *Larchfield*, which featured the poet W. H. Auden, was published in 2017. She is now the Literature programmer at Cove Park, Scotland, dividing her time between Scotland and a London house boat.

Friends is on page 47.

Gillian Clarke (born 1937)

Gillian was born in Cardiff to Welsh-speaking parents, though she grew up speaking English and only later learned Welsh herself. She has written many poetry collections for adults and children, as well as plays for theatre and radio. She translates poetry and prose from Welsh, and her own work has been translated into ten languages including Chinese. Gillian was the National Poet of Wales from 2008 to 2016. Her prize-winning poems are studied on the GCSE and A-Level syllabus, and she performs regularly for Poetry Live!

Mali is on page 27.

Lucille Clifton (1936–2010)

Lucille grew up in Buffalo, New York, though she moved to Baltimore in 1967. She held many professorships and fellowships and was Maryland's

Poet Laureate from 1974 to 1985. She wrote numerous books covering subjects including family relationships, the struggle for civil rights, black political leaders, women poets, the legacy of slavery, women's history, terrorism and her struggle with breast cancer. The girls in her family were born with an extra finger on each hand which was amputated in childhood, and she often wrote about her 'ghost fingers' and their activities. Lucille also wrote many much-loved children's books.
Homage to my Hips is on page 163.

Kristina Close

Kristina has a Canadian voice but was born in the UK. Her poems have appeared in various magazines and anthologies including *Poetry Wales*, *Rialto* and *Magma*. Her poem, 'Gone', won the 2016 Cheltenham Buzzwords competition.
And then he said: When did your arms get so big? is on page 165.

Mary Elizabeth Coleridge (1861–1907)

Mary was the great-great-niece of Romantic poet Samuel Taylor Coleridge, but was better known during her life for her eerie, imaginative novels. She was too shy to publish her poetry under the famous family name, so she did so under the pseudonym 'Anodos'. Her poetry only reached a wide audience after her death when another poet, Henry Newbolt, published them under her real name. Mary never married, and devoted most of her time to lecturing at the Working Women's College in London.
A Moment is on page 65.

Vittoria Colonna (c. 1490–1547)

Vittoria was from a noble family and was the most admired female poet in Italy during her lifetime. Her husband spent most of his time

away at war and they had no children. When he was killed in battle, she defied her family, and even the Pope, by refusing to marry again, instead moving into a Roman convent as a guest rather than a nun. Her reputation for being devout and chaste helped her avoid the accusations of being 'fame-hungry' that were often aimed at women who published their work at the time. Vittoria was respected by leading writers and artists, including Michelangelo, who was at her side when she died and wrote that 'tears were in all eyes'.
The Juniper Tree is on page 194.

Abigail Cook (born 1997)

Abigail received a scholarship to the Guildhall School of Music and Drama and was a 2015 SLAMbassadors performance winner. She writes frankly about mental health, family, her body and sexuality, and leads workshops in poetry and performance. She was included in the anthology *Rising Stars*, which was Highly Commended in the 2018 CLiPPA.
My Body is on page 164.

Susan Coolidge (1835–1905)

Susan's real name was Sarah Chauncey Woolsey and she is best remembered as the author of the children's book *What Katy Did*, with Katy's family modelled on her own lively, well-off New England clan. It has been a great favourite with many generations of children, including the author Jacqueline Wilson, who wrote her own book *Katy* in tribute. Sarah worked as a nurse during the American Civil War (1861–1865) and it was after this experience that she started to write poems, short stories and fiction for adults and children.
New Every Morning is on page 131.

Wendy Cope (born 1945)

Wendy wasn't fond of the 'fairies and nature' poems she learned at school, but loved it when her father recited 'The Charge of the Light Brigade' to her. In her bestseller *Making Cocoa for Kingsley Amis*, she mocked the literary establishment in the shape of a dreadful fictional poet called Jason Strugnell, and her pitch-perfect parodies have won her many fans. She also edits anthologies and writes poems for children. She was awarded an OBE in 2010.

The Orange is on page 130.

Frances Cornford (1886–1960)

Frances was Charles Darwin's granddaughter and grew up in a lively, well-educated extended family near Cambridge. Her husband – also a poet – was called Francis so they were known by their initials FCC and FCD to avoid confusion. They had five children, one of whom became a poet himself but was killed fighting in the Spanish Civil War. She published eight books of poetry. 'To a Fat Lady Seen from the Train' was her most well-known poem, and was so famous that it was even parodied by G. K. Chesterton and A. E. Housman.

Ode on the Whole Duty of Parents / The Guitarist Tunes Up are on pages 7 and 68.

Yrsa Daley-Ward (born 1989)

Yrsa grew up in Lancashire, where she felt her West Indian and West African heritage made her an outsider. She worked as a model in London and, later, in Cape Town, where she also began to write and perform poetry. Her first collection, *Bone*, was initially self-published before being snapped up by Penguin Books, and she has also published short stories and *The Terrible*, a memoir. Yrsa has written movingly about depression and mental health and her poetry has won

her a large and enthusiastic following online.
heat is on page 191.

Jan Dean (born 1950)

Jan runs workshops in schools, libraries and even cathedrals, encouraging people to write. She has published children's fiction and poetry collections including the CLiPPA shortlisted *Wallpapering the Cat*. She says, 'Writing poems is wonderfully strange – like playing lucky dip with a barrelful of tigers, raspberry jellies and machine parts.' Her poem 'Rosa Parks' celebrates the civil rights activist who refused to give up her seat to a white passenger on a bus in 1955, which made her a key inspiration to the movement.
Three Good Things / Rosa Parks are on pages 143 and 182.

Imtiaz Dharker (born 1954)

Imtiaz was born in Lahore but moved to Glasgow at the age of one. She calls herself a Scottish Muslim Calvinist, adopted by India and married into Wales. Also an artist, she illustrates her prize-winning poetry herself and has exhibited her drawings around the world. She is also a documentary maker and has produced films for Indian organizations working to combat homelessness and promote women's rights and education.
How to Cut a Pomegranate / Flight Radar are on pages 14 and 24.

Emily Dickinson (1830–1886)

Emily was from an upper-crust Massachusetts family and was apparently a sociable girl until something – scholars are divided about whether this might have been an unrequited love affair, or mental health struggles – led her to withdraw from the world. She retreated into the house, dressed all in white, and wrote almost 2,000 passionate poems which were discovered after her death. Some were neatly bound in little books, while others were scribbled on envelopes and the recipes she loved to cook. Only a handful were published before Emily's death, and early editions 'corrected' her unusual punctuation. It wasn't until 1955 that they appeared in print as she had written them, but she is now acknowledged to be one of history's most important and best-loved poets.

There is No Frigate Like a Book / *'Hope' is the Thing with Feathers* / *Behind Me – dips Eternity* are on pages 144, 174 and 215.

H.D. (Hilda Doolittle) (1886–1961)

In 1911 H.D. left her native America for a holiday and never returned. In England, she met the poet Ezra Pound – to whom she was briefly engaged – and he became her champion, admiring her poems for their 'straight talk'. A leading member of the Imaginists, she wrote stripped-down free verse in contrast to the more flowery poetry that had come before. She suffered a breakdown after her marriage (to another poet, Richard Aldington) collapsed, her father died and her brother was killed in the First World War, and in the early 1930s she was psychoanalysed by Sigmund Freud himself in Vienna. To aid her recovery, H.D. moved to Corfu with her lover Annie Ellerman (who wrote novels under the name Bryher) and there saw visions of the Greek gods. She later wrote several feminist takes on ancient myths including the Trojan War.

The Moon in Your Hands is on page 140.

Lady Dorothea Du Bois (1728–1774)

Dorothea's father, the Earl of Anglesey, was evidently something of a cad. He declared his marriage to Dorothea's mother invalid due to a previous entanglement, making his three daughters, including Dorothea, illegitimate. Dorothea's mother pursued him through the courts but never saw a penny of the money he was ordered to pay her, and his estate passed to the son of his third wife. This sorry saga was told in several of Dorothea's books, including *Poems by a Lady of Quality*, which she hoped in vain might secure her justice. She married a French musician and had six children, eventually dying penniless in Dublin.

Song is on page 21.

Carol Ann Duffy (born 1955)

Carol Ann was born in Glasgow. She grew up in Stafford and then attended the University of Liverpool, where she studied Philosophy. She has written for both children and adults, and her poetry has received many awards, including the Signal Prize for Children's Verse, the Whitbread and Forward Prizes, as well as the Lannan Award and the E. M. Forster Prize in America. In 2009 she became Poet Laureate. In 2012 she was awarded the PEN Pinter Prize.

Valentine is on page 63.

Helen Dunmore (1952–2017)

Helen wrote children's books, novels – including *Birdcage Walk* – and criticism about Emily Brontë and Virginia Woolf, as well as poetry. She had a house in Cornwall and was an intrepid sea swimmer, braving the waves in a wetsuit on cold days. Her final poetry collection *Inside the Wave* was published just before she so sadly died from cancer, and it posthumously won the Costa Poetry and Book of the Year awards in 2017.

September Rain is on page 210.

Rhian Edwards

Rhian studied Law, and worked as a tax consultant and selling advertising for the *Financial Times* before meeting a group of poets in London who inspired her to take up writing herself. Also a singer-songwriter who performs on stage and for radio, she is now an award-winning poet. She lives in South Wales with her daughter.

Polly is on page 39.

George Eliot (1819–1880)

Mary Ann Evans published under a male pseudonym because she wanted her novels – which include *Middlemarch* and *The Mill on the Floss* – to be taken seriously, but also because of her personal life. She lived with George Henry Lewes, who was married (though his wife had children with another man). Although affairs were not uncommon, their openness was. It was the cause of a decades-long rift with her brother Isaac – to whom her 'Brother and Sister' sonnets are addressed, some twenty years after they were estranged.

School Parted Us [extract from 'Brother and Sister' Sonnets] is on page 10.

Rebecca Elson (1960–1999)

A distinguished Canadian-American astronomer, Rebecca was one of the world's leading researchers into star clusters and galaxy formation. She also climbed mountains on three continents, spoke three languages, played the mandolin, cooked wonderfully and was a star striker in her Saturday League football team. In 1996 she married Italian artist Angelo di Cintio. Rebecca was diagnosed with non-Hodgkins lymphoma at the age of twenty-nine, and although she went into remission, it eventually returned and she died tragically young, aged thirty-nine.

Antidote to the Fear of Death is on page 148.

'Ephelia'

Ephelia's true identity is unknown, though she is presumed to have been living in London during the 1670s and 1680s. In 1679 she published

Female Poems on Several Occasions, one of the earliest collections of poems written from a female perspective. Some of the poems suggest she was jilted by a lover, leading the feminist scholar Germaine Greer to suggest that she might have been Cary Frazier, the Earl of Mulgrave's rejected mistress. She was possibly well-connected at the court of Charles II, since her poems certainly circulated intellectual circles there. Maureen E. Mulvihill has made a case for her to have been Mary Villiers, later the Duchess of Richmond.
To a Proud Beauty is on page 156.

Catherine Maria Fanshawe (1765–1834)

Catherine was a wealthy socialite whose father was a leading nobleman at the court of George III. Her family were supportive of her interests in art and writing but she didn't publish her poetry during her lifetime, instead circulating copies among her well-connected friends. Her work, including a jaunty parody of William Wordsworth, was published after her death. She wrote a famous 'Riddle on the Letter H', though it has often been misattributed to the Romantic poet Lord Byron.
When Last We Parted is on page 51.

Elaine Feinstein (born 1930)

Elaine has written novels, radio and television drama and biographies, including those of poets Ted Hughes and Marina Tsvetaeva. She is also a translator and award-winning poet. Born in Liverpool, she went to Cambridge University in 1949, only a year after women were first granted full admission. She is married with three sons, and was awarded a Civil List pension in 2005 in recognition of her services to literature.
Anniversary is on page 79.

Rachel Field (1894–1942)

Rachel wrote plays, novels and collaborations with her husband, but was best known as a writer for children. She spent her summers in Cranberry Isles in Maine, which almost certainly inspired her poem 'If Once You Have Slept on an Island'. She also wrote the English lyrics for the version of 'Ave Maria' that appears in Disney's *Fantasia*. Rachel died of pneumonia caught after an operation aged only forty-eight.
If Once You Have Slept on an Island is on page 132.

Kathleen Fraser (born 1937)

Kathleen moved to New York to work for *Mademoiselle* magazine before becoming a poet. She taught poetry in San Francisco from the 1970s to the 1990s, and lobbied for more women writers to be included on the curriculum. She founded the American Poetry Archives and between 1983 and 1991 edited *HOW(ever)*, a journal devoted to suporting women's writing. She divides her time between San Francisco and Rome.
Poem In Which My Legs Are Accepted is on page 166.

Victoria Gatehouse (born 1970)

A Yorkshire poet, Victoria originally trained as a scientist and works as a clinical researcher. She has a Masters degree in poetry from Manchester Metropolitan University and has won several poetry competitions. Her first pamphlet, *Light After Light*, was published in 2018.
Phosphorescence is on page 58.

Nikita Gill (born 1987)

Nikita was born in Belfast but grew up in New Delhi, where an inspiring teacher encouraged her to publish a short story about her grandfather in a newspaper. She has gained an enormous online following, and her first collection, *Wild Embers*, was published in 2017. Nikita has written about her experiences of being bullied, unhappy and abusive relationships, and mental health, as well as poems with a feminist slant inspired by Greek myths.

93 Percent Stardust is on page 197.

Chrissie Gittins

Chrissie worked as an artist and teacher before starting to write full-time. She has written poetry for adults and children, short stories and radio drama – including a play about a dinner party served in the mould of a life-sized iguanodon. Chrissie has been a writer in residence at schools, libraries and Belmarsh Prison. You can hear Chrissie reading her poems on the Poetry Archives.

The Unseen Life of Trees is on page 106.

Remi Graves (born 1992)

Remi is a London-based poet and drummer. Her work has been featured at St Paul's Cathedral, on BBC Radio 4 and more. She runs poetry workshops in schools and libraries and loves helping young people share their own stories. Remi was a National Poetry Day Ambassador in 2017. She is also Elmo's biggest fan.

It Is Everywhere is on page 128.

Dora Greenwell (1821–1882)

Dora was often ill and never married, living instead with her mother and, later, her brothers. She wrote many religious poems, some of which were set to music as hymns. She also wrote in passionate support of women's suffrage and education and against the slave trade. Dora had friends among the literary celebrities of the day, including Christina Rossetti, and it is thought that she had an opium habit.

A Scherzo: A Shy Person's Wishes is on page 158.

Laura Grey (1889–1914)

Laura Grey was the stage name of Joan Lavender Baillie Guthrie, an idealistic young suffragette whose suicide shocked society. Lavender, as she was known, acted on the London stage until she was arrested for window-breaking during the campaign to win votes for women. She was jailed in Holloway Prison with other suffragettes, including Emily Wilding Davison, and force-fed after a hunger strike. While there, she wrote a poem, 'To D. R.' (thought to be fellow campaigner Dorothea Rock), that was published as part of an anthology called *Holloway Jingles* by the Women's Social and Political Union. Lavender was released after four months but her health never recovered, and she began to rely on tranquillizers. Her mother was desperately worried about her mental state, but was unable to get Lavender the help that might have prevented her tragic death.

To D. R. is on page 41.

Hadewijch of Antwerp (thirteenth century)

We know little about Hadewijch's life, except that she was a visionary and poet writing in the thirteenth century who probably lived in Antwerp. Some of her poems are attributed to 'Hadewijch II' as there were two groups of works with different handwriting discovered among her papers. She was presumably aristocratic, since she was highly educated and fluent in Dutch, Latin and French. Hadewijch wrote religious poems using the traditions of love poetry. Her letters suggest she spent some time in a 'beguine' house – these were refuges for religious women who took vows of poverty and chastity but didn't become nuns – and, later, travelled.

You Who Want is on page 141.

About the Poets

Anne Halley (1928–2004)

Anne, christened Ute Halle, was born in Germany, but the Nazi regime banned her father from practising medicine because he was Jewish and the family moved to America, settling in New York in 1938. She taught English, as well as writing poetry and short stories, and translating German works. Disparaging editorial comments on her work from male editors – 'all that kitchen sink imagery!' and 'too much female self-pity' – cemented her commitment to feminism.
A Pride of Ladies is on page 60.

Sue Hardy-Dawson (born 1963)

Sue is a poet and artist who has been widely published in children's anthologies. Before becoming a poet she was a family support worker and teaching assistant – Sue has dyslexia and is passionate about encouraging children with special educational needs. She runs multi-sensory poetry workshops for children of all ages. Sue's wonderful collection *Where Zebras Go* was shortlisted for the 2018 CLiPPA and *Apes to Zebras*, co-written by Roger Stevens and Liz Brownlee, is out now.
Diaspora is on page 2.

Frances Ellen Watkins Harper (1825–1911)

Frances was born in Baltimore to a free African American couple. She was raised by her activist uncle after her mother's death, and worked all her life to promote women's rights and education as well as civil rights. A hundred years before Rosa Parks, she refused to give up her seat in the section of a segregated trolley car in Philadelphia reserved for white passengers. She lectured and wrote against slavery and helped slaves flee to Canada via the Underground Railroad. Frances was married with three step-children and a daughter of her own.
Eliza Harris is on page 179.

Kaylin Haught (born 1947)

Kaylin was born in Illinois and raised on the Oklahoma prairie. Her father worked on an oilfield and was also a preacher, and her mother was a factory worker and Sunday School teacher. 'God Says Yes To Me' has been widely anthologized, and even set to jazz.
God Says Yes To Me is on page 198.

Winifred Holtby (1898–1935)

A feminist, socialist, pacifist and campaigner against racism, Winifred once wrote that a 'passion for imparting information to females appears to be one of the major male characteristics', spotting instances of 'mansplaining' over seventy years before the word was coined. In 1931 she was diagnosed with Bright's disease and given two years to live, and she poured all the energy of her last months into writing *South Riding*. Although better known during her life for her journalism, it is this last novel for which she is now best remembered.
Boats in the Bay is on page 142.

Anne Hunter (1742–1821)

The daughter of a Scottish surgeon, Anne married another surgeon: John Hunter, whose collection formed the basis for London's Hunterian Museum of medical artefacts. Her sparkling parties (of which her husband didn't always approve) attracted literary London's superstars, including the so-called 'Bluestockings': educated women who discussed intellectual matters despite disapproval from male critics of the time. Her poetry was published anonymously at first, and then as Mrs John Hunter, and often concerned romantic or domestic matters. In an age without trains or telephones, and when childbirth was so dangerous for women, Anne was understandably upset when her daughter moved away from home with her new husband.

To My Daughter On Being Separated from Her on Her Marriage is on page 23.

Jean Ingelow (1820–1897)

Jean's poems and novels sold well, and leading Victorian poets Alfred, Lord Tennyson, and Christina Rossetti were among her fans. She threw dinner parties for her poorer neighbours several times a week, funded by the sale of her books – she was apparently very skilful at carving a roast. She also wrote hymns and children's stories.
Seven Times One: Exultation is on page 134.

Lesley Ingram

Lesley was born in Yorkshire and has researched ekphrasis as translation. She has worked in IT, dabbled in archaeology, been a tax officer and taught English in France. She has performed her poems at literary and poetry festivals, and enjoys photographing floors, walls and ceilings, including carpets of bluebells and sandy beaches. She loves liquorice and graveyards.
The Pale Horse is on page 29.

Elizabeth Jennings (1926–2001)

Elizabeth worked briefly in publishing and as a librarian before becoming a full-time writer, living most of her life in Oxford. Her Roman Catholicism and experience of mental breakdown in the 1960s both influenced her verses. Although she disliked reading her poems in public, she became a mentor to student poets, and frequently welcomed them into her ornament-cluttered flat for discussion and tea. She was an avid consumer of ice cream and a keen cinema-goer.
Friendship is on page 44.

Jenny Joseph (1932–2018)

Jenny was a writer of poetry, prose and children's books, and worked as a lecturer, journalist, cleaner, pub landlady, and for an anti-apartheid magazine in South Africa. Her best known poem 'Warning' is about ageing disgracefully and was written when she was only twenty-eight. It became enormously popular and was twice voted the UK's favourite postwar poem, inspiring many fans and imitators around the world. She admitted to mixed feelings about its runaway success, but her many other poems are now also widely enjoyed.

The Sun Has Burst the Sky / Warning are on pages 72 and 199.

Jackie Kay (born 1961)

Jackie had a Scottish mother and Nigerian father, but was brought up by white adoptive parents, which inspired her prize-winning first poetry collection *The Adoption Papers*. She has written plays, children's books and television dramas – though she once admitted to hiding from her publisher under a table because one of her books was taking so long to write. Jackie is the third modern Makar (the Scottish Laureate). 'Fiere' is dedicated to Jackie's best friend Ali Smith and was inspired by the Robert Burns poem 'John Anderson my Jo', which traces the long lifetime of a marriage in just two stanzas. 'Fiere' takes three stanzas to follow a friendship through a lifetime.

Fiere is on page 53.

Amineh Abou Kerech

Amineh is from Damascus. She arrived in Oxford in 2016 after a long exile in Egypt and energetically set about learning English and getting to the top of every class with her sister. She writes all the time, in Arabic and in English, and is forever calling up her homeland.

To Make A Homeland is on page 3.

Rukiya Khatun

Arriving in the UK at the age of six, Rukiya worked with enormous determination to qualify as a lawyer in 2017. Her poems take inspiration from the landscapes and language of her home country, Bangladesh. *Sylhet* is on page 112.

Else Lasker-Schüler (1869–1945)

Else was a German Jewish poet and playwright. She moved to Berlin with her first husband where she trained as an artist, published her first poems, had a son and became renowned for her alternative lifestyle. Her poems were successful and influential, but after marrying and separating from her second husband and the death of her son, she found herself penniless and suffered from depression. She fled the Nazi regime and eventually settled in Jerusalem.
Reconciliation is on page 74.

Emma Lazarus (1849–1887)

Emma was from a Jewish family in New York. She worked on Ellis Island teaching English to Jews who had fled persecution in Russia, and wrote passionately against anti-Semitism. 'The New Colossus' was written to raise funds to build a pedestal for the Statue of Liberty (the statue itself was a gift to America from France) and it was eventually inscribed upon the monument itself.
The New Colossus is on page 175.

Mary Leapor (1722–1746)

Mary's father was a Northamptonshire gardener and, despite her lack of education, she had great writing ambitions: from childhood she 'would often be scribbling and sometimes in rhyme'. As a domestic servant she was lucky with one employer – Susanna Jennens was a poet herself, encouraged Mary's writings and let her educate herself in her library – but less so with another, who fired her for writing while his dinner burned. Mary died of measles aged only twenty-four, never having seen her work in print. Her poems, published after her death, protested against the difficulties she faced as a working-class woman, and criticized the way society valued women only for their looks and fortunes.

Extract from *Essay on Friendship* is on page 45.

Jean Little (born 1932)

Though Canadian poet Jean Little was born legally blind, it hasn't stopped her writing poetry, children's books, novels and her autobiography. She taught disabled children and her first children's book featured a child with cerebral palsy. Jean has six honorary degrees and is a Member of the Order of Canada. She lives in Ontario with her sister, great-niece and great-nephew, and her guide dog, Honey.

Today is on page 136.

Pippa Little

Born in Tanzania and raised in Scotland, Pippa now lives in Northumberland. She has travelled extensively in central Europe and translated Hungarian and Spanish poetry. She has a PhD in contemporary women's poetry and her collections include *Our Lady of Iguanas*, *The Spar Box* and *Twist*.

Huge Blue is on page 20.

Liz Lochhead (born 1947)

Liz had written poetry since her childhood but before becoming a full-time writer she was – she says – a 'terrible' teacher. She has written songs and plays, as well as poetry, and was the Makar (Scotland's Poet Laureate) from 2011 to 2016. You can also hear her voice on 'Trouble is Not a Place', a track by experimental Glaswegian hip-hop group Hector Bizerk. Liz has said of feminism that it 'is like the hoovering: you just have to keep doing it'.

A Glasgow Nonsense Rhyme for Molly is on page 6.

Amy Lowell (1874–1925)

Amy was from a prominent Massachusetts family who didn't think their daughters should go to college, but fortunately their mansion had a library stocked with 7,000 books. At the age of twenty-eight she decided to become a poet, so she read intensively for eight years in preparation. She was a poetry pioneer and campaigned forcefully to bring it to a wider audience by lecturing, translating and nurturing new talent. A flamboyant and eccentric figure with a pince-nez, bun, and a cigar permanently in hand, Amy became a poetry celebrity. She lived with actress Ada Dwyer Russell, to whom many of her poems are addressed.

A Decade / Wind and Silver are on pages 77 and 123.

Hollie McNish (born 1983)

Hollie has published the poetry collections *Papers*, *Cherry Pie*, and a poetic memoir of parenthood, *Nobody Told Me*, winner of the Ted Hughes Award for New Work in Poetry 2016. She co-wrote the play *Offside*, which relates the two-hundred-year history of UK women's football, and collaborated with the Dutch ensemble, the Metropole Orkest, on her second poetry album *Poetry Versus Orchestra*. McNish tours the UK extensively, and her poetry videos have attracted millions of views worldwide. She has a keen interest in migration studies, infant health and language learning, and gives performances of her work for

organizations as diverse as the *Economist*, MTV and UNICEF.
Milk-Jug Jackers is on page 5.

Katherine Mansfield (1888–1923)

Born Kathleen Mansfield Beauchamp in Wellington, New Zealand, Katherine is better known as a writer of short stories than as a poet. A passionate and, by all accounts, occasionally difficult character, her love-life was rather complicated: while pregnant with the child of another man, she married her much older music teacher, only to abandon him days later. Rushed away to Germany by her scandalized mother, she suffered a stillbirth. Her relationship with her second husband, John Middleton Murry, was more affectionate by letter than in person. The presence of Ida Baker – the woman she called her 'wife' – was presumably a bone of contention. She died of tuberculosis aged only thirty-four.
When I Was a Bird / Camomile Tea / The Awakening River are on pages 9, 75 and 98.

Charlotte Mew (1869–1928)

Charlotte's middle-class family had little money after her father died, and she and her sister Anne worked to contribute to the household. They had another brother and sister who had been certified insane and confined to asylums, and Charlotte and Anne vowed never to marry, to avoid passing on mental illness to their children. She wrestled with her faith throughout her life and in her poems, feeling attracted to Roman Catholicism but never actually converting. The deaths of her mother and Anne devastated Charlotte, and she sadly took her own life.
The Call / May 1915 are on pages 192 and 200.

Alice Meynell (1847–1922)

Despite having eight children, Alice found time to write journalism, as well as poetry, and assist her husband editing journals. She campaigned against animal cruelty, for better living conditions for London's poor, and for votes for women. She also spoke out against oppression as doubts about colonialism and the British Empire began to be felt in the late nineteenth century. The Meynells took in and supported Francis Thompson, a poet who had fallen on hard times due to his opium addiction.

Renouncement is on page 83.

Elma Mitchell (1919–2000)

Elma was a Scottish poet who worked as a librarian for the BBC. She was fluent in languages including Russian and worked as a translator and freelance writer, publishing poetry from the 1960s onwards. She worked in a thatched barn that served as both library and study, and was inhabited by rare bats. Elma read fiercely and brilliantly at her rare public readings, even when she was elderly and frail.

This Poem . . . is on page 145.

Hannah More (1745–1833)

Hannah had a long engagement which was eventually broken off, but she accepted an annuity from the jilter which gave her the financial independence to work on her writing. She campaigned against slavery and was a member of the Bluestockings, an eighteenth-century women's society who gathered to discuss intellectual matters. Hannah established schools for the poor in the west of England, despite resistance from local farmers who worried an educated population wouldn't be content with labouring work, and clergymen who had previously been in charge of education.

Extract from *The Bas Bleu* is on page 49.

Michaela Morgan

Michaela is a children's author and poet who has written more than 140 books. She has visited schools in the UK, Europe, the USA and Africa, and also gives workshops and readings in libraries, at festivals and in prisons. Her latest poetry collections are *Wonderland: Alice in Poetry* and *Reaching the Stars: Poems About Extraordinary Women and Girls* (Macmillan). Michaela is really quite small. But very fierce.

My First Day at School is on page 184.

Pauli Murray (1910–1985)

Anna Pauline Murray was inspired to become a lawyer after being arrested for sitting in the 'whites only' section of a Virginia bus in 1940, and she continued fighting for civil and women's rights all her life. She faced prejudice throughout her studies because of her gender and race, but eventually became California's first black attorney general. Her 1950 book *States' Laws on Race and Color* was a key contribution to the civil rights movement, and she was appointed to the Presidential Commission on the Status of Women by John F. Kennedy in 1961. Pauli had a brief marriage to a man, which was annulled, and several relationships with women.

Ruth is on page 195.

Eileen Myles (born 1949)

Eileen Myles are a poet, novelist, performer and art journalist. Their twenty books include the upcoming *Evolution*, *Afterglow (a dog memoir)*, *Cool For You*, *I Must Be Living Twice/new & selected poems*, *Inferno* and *Chelsea Girls*. In 1992 Myles ran an openly female write-in campaign for President of the United States. They live in Marfa TX and New York.

Uppity is on page 146.

Edith Nesbit (1858–1924)

Edith wrote many books, and is especially remembered for her much-loved children's stories, including *Five Children and It*, *The Phoenix and the Carpet* and *The Railway Children*. She had a tempestuous personal life with her husband Hubert Bland – they both had affairs, and Hubert had children with other women, some of whom Edith brought up as her own. She co-founded the socialist Fabian Society.
Among His Books / The Things That Matter are on pages 84 and 212.

Grace Nichols (born 1950)

Grace was born in Guyana, and moved to Britain in 1977. Her first book, *I is a Long-Memoried Woman*, won the Commonwealth Poetry Prize in 1983, and she has also written stories and poems for children and a novel. She is inspired by folklore and Caribbean rhythms and culture. Grace has edited anthologies of poetry and was poet in residence at the Tate Gallery from 1999 to 2000.
For Forest is on page 110.

Selina Nwulu

As well as a poet, Selina is a writer and campaigner in the areas of social justice, politics, education and the environment who has worked for non-profit organizations, including UN Women and the Equality and Human Rights Commission. She co-edited *Women's Views on News* and has published widely. Selina was Young Poet Laureate for London in 2015–2016 and has performed around the UK and further afield.
Tough Dragons is on page 162.

Mary Oliver (born 1935)

Mary's poems are filled with a wonder at the natural world she felt from childhood, when she loved to walk in her native Ohio and wrote poetry from the age of fourteen. Mary lived in Massachusetts for many years with her long-term partner and literary agent Molly Malone Cook, and has written many poems inspired by the Cape Cod coastline. Mary's poems have won numerous awards, including the Pulitzer Prize, and the *New York Times* called her 'far and away America's best-selling poet'. *Breakage* is on page 103.

Alice Oswald (born 1966)

Alice Oswald studied Classics at Oxford and then trained as a gardener. She worked in gardens for seven years before publishing her first book of poems, *The Thing In the Gap-Stone Stile*, which won the Forward Prize in 1996. Her latest collection, *Falling Awake*, was shortlisted for the Forward Prize for Best Collection and the T. S. Eliot Prize 2016, and was the winner of the Costa Poetry Award 2016. In June 2017 she was awarded the International Griffin Poetry Prize. She is married with three children and lives in Devon.
Wedding is on page 78.

Dorothy Parker (1893–1967)

Wisecracking Mrs Parker grew up in New York and wrote for, among others, *Vogue* and *Vanity Fair*. She became the queen bee of the Algonquin Hotel Round Table, a witty group who met daily for lunch in the hotel on West 44th Street to bitch, drink, gossip and generally congratulate themselves. It was a glamorous new world – women were drinking, carrying on with men and even, Heaven forbid, dancing the Charleston – but Parker's cool verse often tots up the bitter costs of these freedoms.
Lullaby / Inventory are on pages 155 and 196.

About the Poets

Sylvia Plath (1932–1963)

Sylvia was fiercely ambitious and worked tirelessly on her poetry. She attempted suicide in 1953 and her experiences recovering in a clinic inspired her only novel, *The Bell Jar*. In 1956 she met poet Ted Hughes while studying at Cambridge University. They married and had two children, but she struggled to find time to write with young children to care for and a house to run, and her career stalled while his took off. The relationship broke down and a distraught Sylvia plunged into a creative frenzy, getting up at dawn to write the furious poems for which she is best remembered. She took her own life during the freezing February of 1963. Her first poetry book had appeared in 1960, and *Ariel*, the collection that cemented her extraordinary reputation, appeared two years after her death.

Metaphors / Mirror are on pages 4 and 160.

Wendy Pratt (born 1978)

Wendy is a fully qualified microbiologist, as well having degrees in English Literature and Creative Writing, and is working towards a PhD in poetry. She has published several collections of verse and writes features for publications including *Yorkshire Life*. Her latest collection, *Gifts the Mole Gave Me*, was published by Valley Press in 2017.

Nan Hardwicke Turns Into a Hare is on page 117.

Kathleen Raine (1908–2003)

Kathleen was inspired by the Scottish ballads passed down her mother's family and by her father's love for poetry. She attracted many admirers, though she clashed with her parents over some of her suitors, and her chaotic love-life included marriages, children, elopements and affairs about which she felt enormous guilt. She had an unrequited passion for the writer Gavin Maxwell, whose book *Ring of Bright Water* was named

253

after a line in one of her poems, and felt responsible for causing the death of his beloved otter. Kathleen often wrote about religion and spirituality, and her poems were popular in France, the USA and India, as well as Britain.

Heirloom is on page 25.

Shukria Rezaei

Shukria arrived in Oxford at fourteen, a refugee from Taliban persecution of her Hazara people in the Pakistan border regions of Afghanistan. She started writing poems in English almost before she had the words to do so, bringing a gift for imagery from her Persian heritage. She has seen her work published widely, in *Oxford Poetry* among other publications.

A Glass of Tea is on page 12.

Lola Ridge (1873–1941)

Lola moved from Dublin to New York with her mother. Having married and separated from a goldmine owner, she worked as a copywriter, artist's model, factory worker, illustrator and educator, as well as writing poetry inspired by life on the Lower East Side. She and her second husband were socialist activists, taking part in protest marches and holding lively parties in their shabby apartment for other writers. Lola wrote about subjects considered shocking at the time, including race riots, but her book *The Ghetto and Other Poems* made an immediate impact. She was always sickly, though this impression was reinforced by the fact that she lied about her age, so people – including the writer of her *New York Times* obituary – thought she was ten years younger than she actually was when she died.

A Memory / Submerged are on pages 122 and 139.

Christina Rossetti (1830–1894)

In contrast to her brother, the wild-living Pre-Raphaelite artist and poet Dante Gabriel Rossetti, Christina was so religious that she abstained from playing chess or visiting the opera on religious grounds. She remained unmarried, and devoted herself to charity work, her family and poetry. Although she modelled for her brother and other artists, it tended to be for sacred subjects, and she heartily disapproved of some of the Pre-Raphaelites' other muses, including the ill-starred Lizzie Siddal, her brother's obsession and – eventually – his wife. One of her best-loved poems is 'Goblin Market', in which one naughty sister is tempted by sticky enchanted treats.

In an Artist's Studio / A Birthday / The Trees' Counselling / Remember are on pages 66, 71, 104 and 206.

Olive Runner

Olive's poem was published in *Poetry* magazine in September 1918. Almost a hundred years later, it was rediscovered and celebrated as part of the freedom-themed National Poetry Day 2017.

Freedom is on page 137.

Vita Sackville-West (1892–1962)

Vita grew up on the family estate of Knole, in Kent, which she immortalized in her novel *The Edwardians*, but couldn't inherit because she was a woman. She and her husband Harold Nicolson had an unconventional relationship, both having affairs with men and women. Vita's lovers included Violet Keppel, with whom she often ran away for periods of time, and Virginia Woolf, who was inspired by her to write her 1928 novel *Orlando*. It was a difficult time to have same-sex relationships, and Vita struggled with her feelings and the lack of social tolerance. In 1930 Vita and Harold moved to Sissinghurst in Kent and lovingly restored the ruined gardens there. As well as poems, she wrote biographies of women including Joan of Arc and the seventeenth-century writer Aphra Behn.

Extract from *The Land / Full Moon* are on pages 124 and 133.

Sappho (c. 630–c. 570 BC)

Not many facts are known about Sappho's life, but she lived on the Greek island of Lesbos – probably in Mytilene, the island's biggest city – and is thought to have had several brothers, a husband and a daughter. Most of her poems survive only as fragments, some of which were discovered in ancient Egyptian papier-mâché coffins in 1914. We do know that she was praised throughout the ancient world – Plato called her 'the tenth Muse' – and that her image appeared on statues and coins. At a time when most poetry was formal and meant for public performance, Sappho wrote passionately about her private feelings, including love poems addressed to women. It is from her home island of Lesbos that we get the word 'lesbian'.

Long Departure is on page 52.

Elizabeth Siddal (1829–1862)

Elizabeth was working in a hat shop when one of the Pre-Raphaelite painters persuaded her to model for him. John Everett Millais painted her as *Hamlet*'s Ophelia, though she became ill because she remained still and uncomplaining when the lamps warming the bath in which she was posing went out. Painter and poet Dante Gabriel Rossetti fell in love with her and painted her obsessively, perhaps thousands of times. Scandalously, they lived together for eight years before marriage – Rossetti was reluctant to introduce the working-class Lizzie to his aristocratic family, and she constantly feared (with good reason) that younger models would claim his heart. She suffered from depression, poor health and a laudanum addiction, and had to be carried to the church when they eventually married. She died aged only thirty-three. Rossetti buried a manuscript of unpublished poems with her but, seven years later, he had her body dug up to retrieve them for publication. Elizabeth's drawings and paintings were bought by leading critic John Ruskin during her lifetime, but her own poems were only published after her death.

The Lust of the Eyes / Dead Love are on pages 67 and 93.

Di Slaney

Di founded Nottingham marketing agency Diversity and runs poetry pamphlet publisher Candlestick Press. In 2005 she abandoned city life and moved to an ancient farmhouse, sharing it with – at the last count – 170 rescued and rehomed animals. Caring for livestock has taught her valuable lessons about giving goats antibiotics and closing your mouth when you kiss sheep goodnight, and inspired her first poetry collection, *Reward for Winter*, which includes poems from a hen's point of view.

How to knit a sheep is on page 114.

May Riley Smith (1842–1927)

May was born in New York. Her poems became hugely popular when she was middle-aged, and her books included *Sometime, and Other Poems*. She also wrote hymns.

The Child In Me is on page 208.

Stevie Smith (1902–1971)

Christened Florence, Stevie got her nickname from the jockey Steve Donoghue because she was so small. She was mostly brought up by her beloved, fiercely independent aunt (whom she nicknamed 'Lion') and remained single, observing that marriage looked rather tiring. Stevie published poems illustrated with her own quirky doodles, and rather autobiographical novels in which friends – including George Orwell, with whom she may have had an affair – thought they recognized themselves. She was fascinated by death and religion, and her lively readings won her many fans, including Sylvia Plath, who called herself a 'desperate Smith-addict'. Though she often suffered from ill health and sadness, she had a mischievous sense of dark humour that shines through her poems.

Not Waving but Drowning is on page 207.

Edith Södergran (1892–1923)

Edith was a Swedish-speaking Finnish poet born in St Petersburg during a turbulent time for Russia. After her father became ill, her mother supported the family, giving Edith a strongly feminist role model. Edith fell ill herself and was sent to recover in a Swiss clinic where she met and was inspired by several writers. Her modern, distinctly female style of poetry was ahead of its time – critics were unimpressed, though her work became hugely influential after her death from tuberculosis aged only thirty-one.

On Foot I Wandered Through the Solar Systems is on page 129.

Gertrude Stein (1874–1946)

Born in Pennsylvania, Gertrude moved to France in 1903 and became a leading light of the Parisian poetry scene. She and her lifelong companion Alice B. Toklas held parties that attracted writers and artists including Ernest Hemingway, F. Scott Fitzgerald, James Joyce, Henri Matisse and Pablo Picasso. Her very abstract and innovative poetry did not find a wide audience at the time, but her writing has influenced many generations of poets since.

The house was just twinkling in the moon light is on page 73.

Sara Teasdale (1884–1933)

Sara's poetry was hugely successful, and she won the first Pulitzer Prize in 1918 (when it was called the Columbia Poetry Prize). She had many suitors, including a poet, Vachel Lindsay, who felt he couldn't support her financially, so she married and later divorced another man instead. Afterwards, she rekindled her friendship with Lindsay who was by now married with children. Two years after his death, Sara sadly took her own life. Her poem 'There Will Come Soft Rains' has had a varied cultural history – it provides the title for a short story by Ray Bradbury, and is recited by a robot after the apocalypse in the computer game Fallout 3.

Let It Be Forgotten / There Will Come Soft Rains are on pages 94 and 203.

Kate Tempest (born 1985)

Kate was born in London in 1985. Her work includes the plays *Wasted*, *Glasshouse* and *Hopelessly Devoted*; the poetry collections *Everything Speaks in its Own Way* and *Hold Your Own*; the albums *Everybody Down, Balance* and *Let Them Eat Chaos*; the long poems *Brand New Ancients* and *Let Them Eat Chaos*; and her debut novel, *The Bricks that Built the Houses*. She was nominated for the Mercury Music Prize for her debut album, *Everybody Down*, and received the Ted Hughes Award and a Herald Angel Award for *Brand New Ancients*. Kate was also named a Next Generation poet in 2014.

Thirteen is on page 35.

Jean Tepperman (born 1945)

Jean has worked for most of her life as an editor at alternative and advocacy publications including the *Dorchester Community News*, the *San Francisco Bay Guardian* and *The Children's Advocate*. Now retired, she continues journalism as a freelance reporter. An activist since the age of sixteen, she has always tried to use writing as a tool for building a mass movement for radical social change. In 1975, over forty years before the #MeToo movement, she compiled a book called *Not Servants, Not Machines*, in which female office workers spoke about pay inequality, race and sex discrimination and harassment at work.

Witch is on page 37.

Katharine Towers (born 1961)

Katharine's poetry collections have won several awards and one of the poems from *The Floating Man* was selected as a Poem on the Underground in London. Her second collection *The Remedies* contains a sequence which imagines that the flowers that inspired Dr Edward Bach's 1930s health remedies were each afflicted with the problem they are thought to cure. Katharine lives in the Peak District with her husband and two daughters.

Nerval and the Lobster is on page 116.

Sojourner Truth (1797–1883)

When she was nine, Sojourner was sold as a slave and she had several owners before securing her freedom. She took a slave owner to court in 1828 to win back custody of her son, becoming the first black woman to win such a case against a white man. Sojourner joined organizations working for civil and women's rights and she lectured in front of audiences around America, giving a famous speech in Ohio in 1852. This poem was written later, using a Southern dialect, though in fact Sojourner was from New York, and Dutch was her first language.

Ain't I a Woman? is on page 176.

Alice Walker (born 1944)

Born in rural Georgia, Alice is blind in one eye after an air-gun accident when she was a child. She met Martin Luther King Jr as a student, and has spent her life campaigning for civil and women's rights. After being arrested for a protest at the White House on the eve of the Iraq War, she wrote the essay 'We Are the Ones We Have Been Waiting For'. Alice also wrote the Pulitzer Prize-winning novel *The Color Purple*, which has been filmed and turned into a Broadway musical.

Before I Leave the Stage is on page 193.

Mary Webb (1881–1927)

Mary grew up in Shropshire where her father, a teacher, inspired in her a love of reading and the countryside, and she set her novels there. They have been called 'soil and gloom' books – typically, a tragedy unfolds among simple farming folk – and are brilliantly mocked in Stella Gibbons's *Cold Comfort Farm*.

Why? / Green Rain are on pages 87 and 193.

Anna Wickham (1883–1947)

Born Edith Alice Mary Harper, Anna moved between Australia, France and the UK – her pseudonymous surname inspired by a Brisbane street. Her possessive husband tried to put an end to her singing and writing career, which led to a breakdown and a brief spell in an asylum. Anna published several collections of poetry which were hugely popular, especially in America, and she had many literary friends, including Katherine Mansfield and H.D. Those friendships, however, were sometimes tempestuous: she was rumoured to have once thrown poet Dylan Thomas out of her house during a snowstorm.

A Poet Advises a Change of Clothes is on page 161.

Ella Wheeler Wilcox (1850–1919)

Born to Wisconsin farmers, Ella wrote to support her family. Her mildly steamy poems were hugely popular with readers, though critics snobbishly included her poems in some anthologies of 'worst poems'. During the First World War, Ella believed that her husband instructed her from beyond the grave to visit the Allied Forces in France to boost morale, which she duly did, reciting poems to the troops.
Protest is on page 178.

Helen Maria Williams (1759–1827)

Helen supported the abolition of slavery and praised the French Revolution – both controversial views at the time. She braved the journey to Revolutionary Paris alone, but was imprisoned there for her political writing during the Reign of Terror and, later, by Napoleon, who declared her 'Ode on the Peace of Amiens' to be treasonous.
To Mrs K., On Her Sending Me an English Christmas Plum-Cake at Paris is on page 42.

Dorothy Wordsworth (1771–1855)

Dorothy was the younger sister of poet William Wordsworth and they were extremely close. There were limited options for unmarried women at the time, so, after a miserable period housekeeping for a relative, Dorothy moved in with William and his wife, who was also a friend of hers. She wrote children's stories and helped William with his poems, but most of her own poetry was only published after her death.
Address to a Child During a Boisterous Winter Evening is on page 100.

Index of First Lines

Index of Poets

Acknowledgements

I want to thank every poet who has allowed me to include their work in this anthology. There has never been a more enjoyable job (even though I cried quite a lot!). Thank you for writing such wonderfully thought-provoking and moving poems. A salute, too, to the women poets of the past who are included here, and the many others I read during my research. Your work has not been forgotten.

Enormous thanks to Gaby Morgan for letting me do this, and making the book better every time she touched it. Thanks also to everyone at Macmillan, especially my publicist Amber Ivatt, marketing guru Kat McKenna, and Simran Sandhu for her tireless work tracking down the most obscure of permissions. Thank you to all my bookish friends – particularly Toby Buchan – for advice and encouragement, and to the whole team at Quercus, especially Olivia Mead for putting up with me talking endlessly about this anthology.

Thanks always to my brave and brilliant parents for their unfailing support. You made parenting look easy, though I now know it isn't. And thanks most of all to my husband Mark, who photocopied like a demon on my behalf, and cooked and child-wrangled while I cloistered myself to finish this anthology: you're great.